THE YOUNG CRICKETER'S
MANUAL

THE YOUNG
CRICKETER'S
MANUAL

By

JACK O'CONNOR

*Former Essex and England All-Rounder
and now Chief Coach at Eton*

First published in 1948

CONTENTS

I

No Easy Road to Success

IN 1921, as a very young cricketer, I was accorded the honour of a place in the Essex County eleven, a position I was able to hold throughout the years until the war brought Championship cricket temporarily to an end in 1939.

To-day, although I play for Buckinghamshire in the Minor Counties competition during August, my playing career is drawing to its final curtain. Nevertheless, my interest in the game is as keen, if not keener, than ever, for my primary concern these days is in the coaching and development of cricket youth, mainly as chief coach at Eton College.

During many happy years in first-class cricket I have been privileged to learn a very great deal about the game, and have acquired a wealth of varied experiences, many of which will be recalled in this book, in the hope that they may prove of benefit to all young players. A cricketer can learn much from actual experience, and it is strange, but very true, that failures usually prove the most forceful lessons, for mistakes bring real experience.

Cricket is a vastly different game now from what it was when as a youth I began to conjure up big ideas about my cricket future. Events haven't always transpired as I pictured they would. Often the finished picture, as opposed to my imagined view of it, disappointed, but whether my experiences have been happy or disillusioning, they have helped to build my career and to give me a comprehensive outlook on the game in general.

1

There is a great and ever-increasing enthusiasm for cricket. There is undisputed evidence of this on the village greens of England; in club cricket; at the Essex County grounds, on some of which I assist in the pre-season coaching of youthful and aspiring players; and in my cricket duties at Eton.

English youth is more cricket-minded to-day than ever it was. There is no doubt about that. As evidence of this, the boys at Eton, whether "freshmen" or seniors, are just as keen on their house matches as they are on the more important games against other schools. You see, it is cricket for the game's sake that matters to these up-and-coming youngsters; the grade is not considered.

The reason for much of this welcome wave of enthusiasm among youth is undoubtedly the increased facilities for boys to play cricket at school and the opportunity to obtain first-class coaching. Most County clubs now organise pre-season coaching classes for schoolboys, but no such opportunity was offered to boys in my young days.

Since the end of the war the Essex club has been inundated with applications from lads anxious to receive coaching at the various County grounds. One morning last year I entered the Chelmsford ground to find a scene reminiscent of the start of an important match. The crowd was composed primarily of boys wanting to avail themselves of coaching at the nets by County players, and I hardly knew where to begin, so great was the enthusiastic throng around the nets.

Coaching schemes for boys must do good to the game in general, and with such enthusiastic interest being shown by youth, and a general desire to acquire expert coaching experience, there need be no qualms about the future of English cricket.

2

Dozens of times during a season I am asked this question by young players:

"How can I become a first-class cricketer?"

It is difficult to give a direct, yet effective answer, for there is no royal road to cricket success. There never has been, and there never will be, but it is possible to offer advice and suggestions to help the young cricketer take the first steps towards success.

Assuming that the youthful cricket aspirant has a fair elementary knowledge of the practical side of the game, two other important attributes are essential if he hopes to make any progress whatever:

1. Determination, or the will to succeed, if you prefer to put it that way; and

2. Genuine concentration on the game both from the playing and the psychological angles.

Physical and mental fitness, which can only come from steady living, are also absolutely vital to any player who hopes to rise above mediocrity.

Reaching the top in cricket is rather like climbing a steep cliff. You ascend step by step; stage by stage. You cut footholds and test them thoroughly before you take the next step upwards.

I feel sure that I should have the agreement of every famous cricketer in this contention. Success does not just happen, like switching on the radio. It calls for hard work, more hard work—and then even harder work, coupled with the temperament to take all the ups and downs as they come.

Success in cricket, or rather the achieving of it, demands one hundred per cent enthusiasm; very real determination; a capacity for learning from your failures; and, granted all these, a few smiles from the goddess of fortune.

3

I wish to make myself quite clear upon this point, I am not suggesting for one moment that any player can rely upon luck alone to take him to the top, but one of the outstanding impressions of my career has been the realisation of the part which fortune—and misfortune—play in cricket success and failure.

There are numerous cases of young players whose cricket lives have been made or marred by one stroke of good or bad fortune. An outstanding performance by a "Colt" in his first innings for his County, for example, will almost certainly make a great difference to his future in the game. Not only will it inspire him, but it will give confidence and encouragement to the men who have made his big chance possible.

Illustrations come readily to mind. One of the best is the "story book" first match experience of Harold Gimblett, the Somerset batsman. It was in a match against Essex at Frome in 1935, and I was privileged to take part in his amazing debut, for I was in the field and saw every stroke of his fine innings.

Somerset won the toss and batted first, but six wickets were down for 107 when young Gimblett walked out to the wickets. It was not an enviable position for a lad receiving his County baptism, yet it did not seem to unnerve Gimblett. He revealed the indomitable skill and unruffled temperament of a tried player and he set about the Essex bowling to such good purpose that in little more than an hour he had reached his hundred.

Not only did he score a century on his first appearance in County cricket, but it proved to be the fastest hundred of that season.

Now Harold Gimblett's debut could have been so different. A "snortèr" as his first ball, a half chance

4

accepted by the field when it might have been dropped, or a doubtful umpire's decision against him, could easily have meant failure. Further opportunity to prove himself or to retrieve his former failure might not have presented itself for a long time—if at all.

One match is not enough to reveal all the latent ability of any young player, for there are so many other factors to be taken into account, but chances in big cricket are always limited and a little luck goes a long way when a youth is on the threshold of his career.

However, no player can have any control over twists of fortune of that nature, but when I state that luck plays an important part in the life of every cricketer, I should hasten to point out that there is the less obvious and more abstract kind of fortune, over which the young player CAN have control, to a degree.

Luck of environment, for instance. If the youthful cricket aspirant has the good fortune to "get in" at an early stage with good cricketers, affording him the chance to play the game seriously, thoughtfully, and with full regard to the real science of the game, his progress will be more in keeping with his personal merits.

The youthful cricketer's environment is a matter which should receive the most careful consideration; but such consideration is not always given or accepted.

While a young cricketer is at school, he is playing serious and competitive cricket. It is not necessarily grim, "poker face" cricket all the time, but it is organised, promoting in every boy the earnest desire to improve and to go all out in the matches in which he plays.

There is a very real danger, however, that, schooldays over, the young player will join a club where the social side and not cricket for cricket's sake is the thing that matters. Those who play the game for the social enjoyment it affords, and for no other reason, may find pleasure in this form of cricket, and no one would deny them that pleasure, but to the aspiring youngster who is anxious to improve and, in due course, to reach the top, "social" cricket is of little use.

The youth with ideals and ambitions must join a club where the cricket played is of a fair standard, where the players are keen, and where there is some degree of seriousness and competitive spirit in the play. For the young player anxious to improve his play with all possible speed there is only one thing worse than joining what I will call a "non-cricket" club. That is not joining a club at all.

I know it is possible, without being a registered member of a club, to obtain a fairly complete programme of matches throughout a season. The unattached or "freelance" cricketer usually can manage to secure games with scratch teams; but in such teams, playing only "friendly" games, there cannot be the same keen purpose and competitive spirit which are to be found in a game between two regular club sides.

The value of team work in cricket is not always appreciated, but it is as essential in cricket as in any other game. Not only is it vital to the success of the side, but a sense of team work can pull the best out of the individual players as well.

No cricketer can put his whole heart into a game if the result doesn't really matter, for the desire for personal success—without which no real progress can be made— is not strong enough. Unless a player throws himself whole-heartedly into the team game, there is unlikely to be any improvement in his individual skill.

6

The player who is continually assisting different sides can never acquire really progressive experience, primarily because there will be no competitive urge for him to "play for his place." Then again, the "scratch" cricketer will have no settled place in the batting order. One week first, the next, maybe, last.

In bowling, too, it is impossible to produce the maximum effect when the fieldsmen are strange to the bowler's habits.

The keen cricketer, the player who hopes to make the top grade, must have regular cricket of the highest possible standard, according to his age and capabilities.

I have tried to practise this throughout my cricket life. In the teams I have played for, and in my choice of environment I may have been fortunate. However, this question of correct cricket environment really depends entirely upon the individual.

The cricketer who has no further ambition than to become the most outstanding member of his own team is hampering rather than helping his personal progress. He should find a better grade team, where he may not be able to shine so brightly. Having gained a place in such a team, he can then strive to emulate his former success. It will not be so easy, but the easy way is not the way to the top in any sport.

It behoves every young cricketer to make the effort to join an established club and thus secure for himself the opportunity to play in cricket of a good standard and develop accordingly. When he has made good in that grade, it will be to his own benefit to advance to a higher grade. Step by step—there is no other way to success in cricket.

II

From Club Team to County Cricket

I HAVE purposely told you little, as yet, about my own playing career, but perhaps this is the right moment to introduce you to the boy who later became a County and England player. I will endeavour to show you how those essentials mentioned in the previous chapter—determination and concentration, plus the attention to correct environment, together with a share of good fortune—played their part in setting my feet on the path that led to some measure of success in the game that has been my whole life.

I was fortunate to be born into a cricketing family. My grandfather was Robert (Bob) Carpenter. I was never privileged to watch him at the wicket, but from all I have heard and read about him, he appears to have been a very great batsman. For some years he regularly opened the innings for Cambridgeshire, his partner being the original Tom Hayward, uncle of the man who became a Surrey and England stalwart and one of the game's most illustrious run-getters.

"Grand-dad" Carpenter was also a member of several of the earliest British teams to visit Australia. That was in the days when players wore heavy moustaches and sideboards and played in collars and ties! (But they were most able cricketers for all that.)

Next on the family list was my uncle, Herbert Carpenter, also known as Bob, who won fame as a really fine opening bat for Essex. In due time came my own father, Jack O'Connor, who spent his best years in cricket as a spin bowler with Derbyshire.

Thus, you see, I inherit my batting from my grand-father and uncle, and my natural spin bowling talent from my father. If I also have shown any particular coaching aptitude, that also may be inborn, for Uncle Bob was the chief Essex County coach for a number of years, whilst my father assisted the development of many fine players at Fenner's, that famous Cambridge nursery of cricket.

I was born at Cambridge quite close to the home of the Hobbs family, and it should not cause you much surprise when I tell you that, living in such an atmosphere of cricket, I nursed one consuming ambition, which was to follow in the family's footsteps.

Cricket was in my blood. From my early schooldays I talked cricket, dreamed cricket, lived cricket.

As a schoolboy I scored my first centuries, and then, in my early 'teens, I realised that if I was to achieve my ambition and become a first-class cricketer, I must join a regular club and gain match experience.

I was fortunate in securing a place in the team repre-senting the New Chesterton Institute at Cambridge, and became an opening batsman, with Syd Hobbs, brother of Jack Hobbs, as my partner. Jack, by then, had begun his long and honoured career with Surrey, after he had been rejected by Essex.

I was fairly successful and had the great pleasure of scoring several more centuries in local matches. That heightened my determination to make cricket my pro-fession. Not that a few hundreds scored in Cambridge club cricket gave me any false ideas of my own ability; my personal opinion of myself was always tempered by

9

the knowledge that I had a very long way to travel before I could hope to emulate those other members of our cricket family.

My father never allowed me to believe that I was better than I was; he was continually emphasising that I had much to learn. How prophetic that advice proved to be. Despite all my years in first-class cricket I have never stopped learning; and to-day I am still learning. It is quite true to say of cricket, as of all other spheres of sport, that no player ever reaches perfection.

There is always something new to learn. Once you have mastered one lesson, another presents itself, and this, too, must be mastered. Step by step—lesson by lesson—yes, that is the only way to cricket success. Slow, maybe, but it is the only sure way.

One of the most gratifying factors of my younger years was that I was allowed to develop my cricketing career on good pitches.

How important this is; more important than many young players seem to realise.

Good cricket CANNOT be played on rough wickets. I am only too well aware that good, true wickets are few and far between in junior and club cricket in this country; I wish the position could be reversed.

No young cricketer can really make progress when he has little opportunity of playing on wickets that are true. This applies to every phase of the game.

How can anyone, for instance, learn the art of batting on a rough pitch? I know that many of you DO score quite an appreciable number of runs on wickets that are far from being perfect, but under such circumstances the runs usually are collected mainly by hitting out at every ball, and not by correct stroke play, which means placing the ball deliberately.

In bowling, too, wickets taken on rough pitches are usually the result of bumps and minor pot-holes which cause the ball to play all manner of tricks, never intended by the bowler.

True pitches force a bowler to use his brains to get his wickets. It is ridiculous for critics of cricket to talk about some of our famous pitches being "made" for big scores and affording the bowler no help. "Too good" they say. But no wicket can be too good for the playing of really worthwhile cricket.

The truer the wicket the harder the bowler must work, co-ordinating his physical skill and his mental power all the time in an effort to dismiss the batsmen when he is afforded little natural assistance from the pitch. But hard work, whether by bowler or batsman, never hurt any cricketer. Without hard work, both muscular and mental, there can be no success.

I deprecate the fact that so many promising young players in this country are forced to train on poor pitches. How can a batsman, for instance, perfect his strokes when one ball shoots straight through and the next gets up and raps him on the shoulder?

Likewise with bowling; what need is there for a bowler to master the arts of swing and spin when he can rely on the diversities of the pitch to gain him wickets?

In my young days I was privileged to play on Parker's Piece, that historic ground at Cambridge, one of the finest stretches of natural turf in the world, the ground where Jack Hobbs and Tom Hayward played their early cricket. On such a wicket I was encouraged to develop my stroke play. If I was dismissed, it was because of my own shortcomings and my lack of experience. It was useless for me to blame the pitch.

At Eton, too, we have some of the finest pitches in the country and anyone who has played on them—even the practice pitches—knows how nearly perfect they are. They certainly give me encouragement and assistance in coaching the boys.

I wish I could impress upon all those connected with junior and club cricket the vital necessity to prepare true wickets. We shall always be handicapped in this country until this side of the game is given more careful attention.

Why is it that so many fine bowlers—and batsmen— are reared on overseas wickets? Perfect pitches for all grades of cricket is the answer. The Australians are always able to produce match-winning bowlers, simply because from boyhood, cricketers "Down Under" are forced to master the arts of the game, knowing that the diversities of the pitch will not take their wickets for them.

I have had personal experience of many of the wickets to be found in the Dominions and Colonies and I have nothing but praise for them. During tours in South Africa and the West Indies and several winters spent coaching in Jamaica I never experienced a bad wicket. There is no cricketer who could say the same of pitches in this country.

If England is to hold its rightful place in the cricket world, the authorities must insist on better wickets for ALL players, wickets on which young players can really do justice to themselves and to their coaches.

So to the aspiring cricketer I would say: always try to practise on good wickets. You will be grateful in later years that you paid attention to this important aspect of your game, for development on true wickets is vital to sure progress.

Having done my best to emphasise the importance of the type of wicket on which you play, let me return to my own career.

I have said already that the player endeavouring to make steady advancement in the game needs, in addition to a fair degree of ability, a certain amount of good fortune. I had no cause to grumble at my own ration of the smiles of fortune.

Having reached a stage in my life when I was more than ever convinced that cricket was my future, I was invited to spend a week's holiday with my uncle, Bob Carpenter, at Leyton. He was then chief coach at the Essex County headquarters. When I accepted that invitation, however, I had no thought of playing any cricket during my stay in London. As a matter of fact, there was no room in my small case for any cricket gear.

Nevertheless, my interest in the game was so keen that I took every opportunity of visiting the County ground. One afternoon two junior games were to be played there, and just before stumps were pitched, the captain of one of the teams asked Uncle Bob if he knew of anyone who would make up their eleven, as they were a man short.

My uncle must have caught a glimpse of me standing over by the pavilion, for he called me across and asked me if I fancied a game.

"I wouldn't mind," I answered, "but as you know I've no flannels or boots with me."

"Don't worry about that," Bob replied. "I'll soon fix you up."

Eventually I found myself turning out with that East London club side. I was a stranger to my team-mates, a substitute enlisted on the spot to make up the necessary number, but it meant a game of cricket to me and nothing else mattered.

I certainly never expected that game to end so surprisingly.

I was sent in fourth wicket down and, feeling in holiday mood, and playing on a very fine wicket, I found the bowling so much to my liking that I was soon hitting the ball all over the Leyton ground. Two balls sailed into the pavilion and when I was eventually caught out, I had collected over sixty runs in quick time.

Among the few spectators of that game, although I was not aware of this or my performance might have been very different, was the County secretary.

I was taking off my pads in the pavilion following my dismissal, when Uncle Bob entered with a stranger, who was introduced to me as the Essex County secretary. I felt somewhat embarrassed by his praise of my recent innings, but my embarrassment changed to utter surprise a moment later when he offered me a trial on the County ground staff.

Here was the chance for which I had dreamed, and it had come to me almost by accident, certainly under sensational circumstances. I needed no persuasion from Uncle Bob to accept that offer.

A few weeks later I left Cambridge to join the staff at Leyton. Soon I was appearing in Essex Club and Ground matches, in which I made several centuries and took a number of wickets.

That early experience, one of the most memorable of my career, is purely personal, of course, and you may be wondering what lesson there is in it for you, my readers. Well, there is one—it is that you should give always of your best on the cricket field, no matter in what grade you are playing, so that if the chance of promotion should come your way—as it did to me—you will be ready to accept it, and thus take your next step up the ladder.

The next step in my own career was my debut in the County Championship eleven.

I have vivid memories of that game. It was against Worcestershire, at Leyton, and while I was padding up prior to taking my place at the wicket for the first time with Essex, and feeling just a trifle nervous, Uncle Bob Carpenter came into the pavilion and gave me some advice which is worth repeating.

"Go out there, Jack," said Bob, "and stay on the middle as long as you can. Runs don't count now, so long as you get acclimatised to the atmosphere of the County game."

What exactly did he mean by that? He was not suggesting that I should adopt a stolid, stay-there-at-any-price policy. In any case, Bob knew that I was a natural batsman and quite capable of using the long-handle when I was set. But this was my debut, my baptism in the highest grade of cricket in which I had played as yet. This was to be the real test of my proficiency.

Bob Carpenter was merely suggesting that I should be careful, that I should feel my way; to walk before I tried to run.

I never forgot that advice, and in the opening match of each new season I repeated the practice of giving myself time to get acclimatised.

Try to appreciate the point of this axiom. By taking things easily for the first few overs, you get accustomed to the middle, and give yourself the chance to concentrate on closely watching the ball, the fielders and the bowlers.

Eventually you begin to feel quite at ease and the shots and the runs come automatically.

An hour on the middle in your first match of the season, or your initial outing in strange company, will do you and your cricket future far more good than having a bang, collecting a few quick runs, and then retracing your steps to the pavilion before you have given yourself the chance to become acclimatised.

Concentration is half the secret of success on the cricket field, especially at the batting crease. But you cannot concentrate if you are back in the pavilion following a swift dismissal—except to concentrate on your misfortune or your failure.

Use the bat to hit the ball by all means (my father encouraged me to do so from my earliest days in school cricket), but do not open up until you are sure of yourself, in other words, until you have become acclimatised to the pace of the wicket, the style and strength of the bowling and the speed of the field.

To return to my debut in the Essex County side. That match taught me several lessons.

Having taken Bob Carpenter's advice and felt my way carefully for a few overs, I managed to score 13 runs. Naturally, as a young player making his County baptism, I was not complete master of my feelings and I must confess that I became a little excited, and a trifle careless, too, I'm afraid.

Down came a tempting ball, I cut it hard and, calling for a run, although it was not MY call, started to scamper down the pitch. At the other end the late Laurie Eastman refused to run and sent me back.

It was too late. The ball had been snapped up by a nimble-fingered fieldsman and whipped back to the

Worcestershire stumper, who had the bails off while I was still scrambling back to my crease.

Run out and, feeling more than a trifle disappointed, I returned to the pavilion to ruminate on my hasty action.

Later on, the Essex skipper, that great all-round cricketer Johnnie Douglas, took me apart and suggested that it would be a good thing if in the future I curbed my impetuosity. He pointed out quite emphatically that my dismissal was entirely my own fault.

"Never attempt a run," said Mr. Douglas, "until the ball has passed the nearest fielder, or at least is well out of his reach."

That first County innings had ended very abruptly, just when I had been feeling that I was set; yet perhaps it was well that it happened as it did, for it taught me lessons that left an indelible impression upon me.

My debut was an experience that helped to mould my future. At that time I had played in hundreds of matches of all sorts, but that initial County game gave me a very definite awareness of my paucity of cricket knowledge.

County cricket was so very different even from senior club cricket. One of my most concrete impressions was the difference in the bowling, especially in the varying pace at which each ball came through. I realised, too, that the bowlers were using their fieldsmen as part of their attacking plan in a way I had never seen before.

I was deeply impressed by the skilful placing of the field and the groundwork of the individual fielders. It was so much keener than anything I had previously experienced. The picking up, the covering, were exceptional, and many times during my first innings in County cricket, when I thought I had put another easy single on the board, I found that I had not.

You will gather that I did not fully appreciate this great difference between club and County cricket until I was back in the pavilion, or I should never have attempted that risky run that resulted in the score card reading: "O'Connor....Run out .. 13."

During the Worcestershire innings I was not called upon to bowl, and when Essex batted a second time my presence was not required at the wickets. Jack Russell, that stylish run-getter of Test fame, with whom I was to spend so many happy hours at the wickets in future years, hit a double century off the Worcester bowlers and the innings was declared closed before my turn came to bat.

When the match had ended and I was able to sit back and recall all that had happened during those three memorable days, I knew without a doubt that I was faced with a very big task if I was to succeed in my new life. I was fully cognisant of my inexperience and I fostered no illusions whatever.

I knew that it would need a complete concentration and co-ordination of mind, limbs and muscles—and all my determination, if I was to make any progress in the County game. Yet I felt confident that with added experience, all the new problems facing me as a County cricketer could be mastered.

All things being equal, the attainment of success in any sphere of life depends to a great extent upon the individual, but there are few players who achieve fame entirely on their own, and here I introduce another word of advice to young cricketers.

Never hesitate to take the advice of older and more experienced cricketers. In this connection I will admit that I was helped over many a stile and across many difficult patches by my County colleagues.

I should like to pay a sincere tribute to Jack Russell, perhaps the finest professional batsman ever to wear the Essex and England caps, for the ready way in which he showed me, during my early days with the County, how I could improve my batting strokes.

Many times he took me into the nets and pointed out how mistakes in my strokes could be rectified by giving me practical demonstration. His coaching efforts on my behalf found full appreciation.

Of course, it is not always possible for the aspiring cricketer to receive such practical coaching from the masters of the game, but often it is not so much what a man says as what he does that leaves the deepest impression. A man's deeds are obvious for all to see, and the endeavour to emulate them is the natural impulse of every young player. So watch the great cricketers and learn all you can from their actual play.

Before I was given that welcome chance to enter County cricket, I took every opportunity to watch the great players of the game when they visited Cambridge; nor did my interest as a spectator cease when I took my place in the County field.

It is impossible to assess the benefit that can be derived from this practice. Whilst serving on the ground staff at Leyton, and later as a "new boy" in the Essex XI, I found the greatest delight in sitting and watching points, noting the brilliant stroke play and the consummate artistry of the super-batsmen of that day, and the methods and wiles of the top grade bowlers.

I watched cricket with the same keen interest as I played it. Even after I had gained a place in the County eleven I watched every ball bowled in every match in which I took part. Whether at the wicket or sitting in the

19

pavilion enclosure, I was always collecting data that could be stored in my memory—the methods and strokes of the master batsmen; the varied deliveries of the leading bowlers; fielding points; in fact every phase of the game afforded me opportunities to increase my fund of knowledge.

I was not alone in that profound interest in cricket as played by the men who were in the top rank when I was just a newcomer to the County side. The late Hedley Verity, that prince of Yorkshire left-arm spinners, whose death during the war came as such an irreparable blow to English Test cricket, used to sit for hours behind Wilfred Rhodes when that other great Yorkshire wizard of spin was in action. Verity learned so well that the time came when he stepped into the shoes of Rhodes with wonderful effect.

I recall the early days of Alf Avery, now an established Essex batsman. As a boy, "Sonny," as he was always known to us, worked in the County office, or at least he should have been working in the office. But when there was a match in progress the face of Sonny Avery was usually to be found glued against the office window so that he could watch the County stars in action.

When, eventually, he was given his chance in the Essex XI, he proved that he had learned a great deal from keeping his eyes open.

Watch the leading players performing and you will find that every match, even though you may not be playing yourself, can be an object lesson, and the example set by the men who have made the grade will prove an incentive to emulation.

There is another very good reason why young players should find profitable pleasure in watching the cricket even when they are not out in the middle. Concentration, as I have said, is one of the most paramount of all the stepping stones to eventual success in any phase of the game, and concentration means keeping your eye on the ball—yes, always.

Whether batting, bowling or fielding, or even watching from the pavilion, I always tried to remember my father's early advice, which was "Never take your eye off the ball for a moment." But that, of course, is a golden rule in any ball game.

III

Be Amenable to Advice

BEFORE DEVOTING special chapters to the arts of batting, bowling and fielding, it might prove interesting and beneficial to detail a few of the good points for which I look in a young player who comes to me for coaching.

The natural cricketer needs little coaching; in fact it is true to say that the development of the majority of young players with a natural, inborn ability, can be hindered rather than helped by coaching that takes no account of instinctive talents.

Overcoaching can be more detrimental than no coaching at all.

Any coach will tell you that it is fatal to attempt to alter a natural style, even although it may not conform to the orthodox code. Such a player must be treated carefully. The coach must endeavour to shape and develop his instinctive style, to advise and suggest rather than offer practical coaching.

The natural player will make his own way in the game, providing he is allowed to develop in the right environment.

Great players like Denis Compton and W. J. Edrich, Len Hutton and Don Bradman, Jack Hobbs and Frank Woolley, needed little coaching in their youth. Each was a "natural" and had any one of them been encouraged to conform to any particular "copy-book" orthodoxy, they might not have developed into the attractive, match-winning players they later became.

As a coach, however, I must admit that I do not meet

many youngsters with such inborn ability that they do not need some degree of moulding. What then do I look for in those whom I am privileged to coach?

I look first to see if the lad has ball sense, an essential in any ball game. Without it he will have no natural knowledge of timing, which means, in other words, that he will have little chance of making the grade in cricket.

I look, too, to see if he knows how to handle a bat. If he knows the half-volley I bowl to him, knows it instinctively, then I label him a "natural." Nevertheless, knowing how to handle a bat is not everything, for even if my young pupil is awkward, with no ease of stance at the wicket, I am not unduly worried. Those faults can be corrected. There are far more important factors which stamp a young player as a future success—or failure.

For instance, is he amenable to coaching? In other words is he ready to accept without question the advice and suggestions his coach has to offer him? The player who objects to being helped along the right road, or who feels that he knows better than his tutor, is only wasting his own time and the time of his coach.

That has happened, and not only in junior circles. There was a very promising young player on a certain county's ground staff who might have become outstanding as an all-rounder, but he showed in no uncertain manner that he resented being told of his faults and mistakes, despite the fact that his mentors were men far more knowledgeable and experienced than he was at that time.

That player did not climb above the ground staff and he vanished from the first-class cricket stage. What a pity.

Another of my tests for the young player—does he show patience? If he does then the pupil will be assured

23

of the reciprocal patience and encouragement of his coach.

Lastly, does he show that degree of determination that is so necessary to the cricketer on the threshold of a career?

Determination, grit, courage—or perhaps you would prefer to term it the will to surmount the obstacles that confront every young player—is often the key to the attainment of success in cricket.

I am reminded of the experience of that very great all-rounder and England Test leader, Johnnie Douglas, under whose captaincy I served with the Essex team. J. W. H. T. was a very poor cricketer during his school-days at Felstead, and my uncle, Bob Carpenter, has told me often that the man who was to skipper his country's cricket forces on Test fields, was hopeless when he first visited Leyton for coaching.

It was dogged determination and a propensity for hard work that made Johnnie Douglas the great player he became. He spent hours, days, weeks trying to assimilate the practical advice of his coaches and he made himself great through his highly-developed will power and his desire to conquer his own failings as a cricketer.

I remember, too, Morris Nichols joining the County staff for a trial as a batsman. At that time Nichols was a tall, ungainly youth with little to commend him except a big heart and an abundance of energy.

Percy Perrin, that prince of Essex amateur batsmen, was watching "Nick" one day batting at the nets and he passed this comment on him:

"He'll make a better fast bowler than a batsman."

In view of this expert opinion, the Essex coaches were told to mould "Nick's" rather crude bowling action in the hope that he might make better use of his natural physical attributes and develop into a speed merchant. It meant long hours of hard and tiring work for the tall youngster, but it is to his credit that he succeeded and in time became one of the greatest fast bowlers this country has seen.

It is quite true that Morris Nichols also blossomed into a very sound batsman, but if it had not been for the patience and the determination of purpose which he displayed in everything he did, plus the perseverance of his coaches, of course, he might never have made the grade in first-class cricket or become such a really solid all-rounder.

Every player who feels that he is not good enough to achieve any success in cricket, can take heart from the actual experiences of others. There are many established County and Test players to-day whose future in cricket looked a little vague, if not hopeless, in their early years, but who triumphed because of their own determination and the patient attention of their coaches.

Such determination and self-control are needed long after a player's "apprenticeship" period. Few cricketers can expect to be always on top of the world. Every player is likely to strike a bad patch at some time during his career, and when this comes it must be faced with fortitude.

Taking a disgruntled view of failure or misfortune will not help matters. To worry about it unduly will certainly not assist the player to recover his form. The reverse is usually the case.

The bad patch must be viewed in its proper perspective and every effort made to surmount it, always remembering that luck runs in cycles. In cricket a man can be right out

c

of form one day and then, without apparent reason, can surprisingly hit the high spots again—that is if he has the grit and the determination to fight back.

I could tell you several instances of players allowing their run of misfortune to affect their play to such an extent that they never recovered and their career was ruined. But the player with the right spirit and the sane outlook will always come again.

The classic case is that of W. J. Edrich. A few years before the war you may remember that he failed time and time again in Test cricket until it seemed that he would never be able to recover the form that had made him one of the most outstanding young batsmen in the country. He refused to give up; his spirit never failed him and, even with the critics unanimous in their opinion that he must be dropped from the Test team, he flashed back to form and recorded a double century in a memorable match against South Africa.

Had Bill Edrich succumbed to that spell of misfortune —and it certainly needed a big heart and dogged determination to "keep his end up" in the face of continued failures—England would have lost one of the finest all-rounders the game has seen this century. But Bill Edrich was built of the right stuff.

It is rather strange that his colleague in so many wonderful partnerships both for England and Middlesex should have had a somewhat similar experience, although not quite so disastrous. I refer to Denis Compton who, during the 1946 season, experienced a period of some weeks when he could do little right with the bat.

Innings after innings saw Compton dismissed cheaply, but never once did he give way to the disappointment he must have felt. Eventually, as a reward for his patient fortitude, his form returned and, having fought his way back to the limelight, Denis Compton became an even greater player, as was proved by his mercurial batting in Tests against Australia and South Africa and in his record-breaking feats with Middlesex.

Misfortunes will come to every cricketer, but the surmounting of a bad patch is an experience that can help to make a man a better player.

Those illustrations were rather out of context, but they serve to show you what an important part determination plays in the life of any young player who hopes to reach the top grade. It is a factor which I look for hopefully in those whom I am privileged to coach.

My coaching experience has shown me that the majority of young players prefer batting to bowling. It seems to be the general opinion that there is more satisfaction, more glory, if you care to put it that way, in scoring a century than taking half a dozen wickets. Well, personal satisfaction is comparative. I am always trying to impress upon the young player that the bowler who can put the other side back in the pavilion is just as worthy a cricketer as the batsman whose efforts enable his side to record a good total on the scoreboard.

In most cases, however, personal preference must be forgotten by the very young player, for it is the coach who is in the best position to decide on which of these two main phases of the game his pupil should concentrate. What happens after the player has developed sufficiently to stand on his own feet and to take his place in senior cricket is not the concern of his former tutor.

Actually, speaking as a coach, I prefer to take over the development of the very young cricketer, from the age of 10 if possible. The boy of tender years is more likely to make rapid progress as he has not acquired fixed habits. The older boy has usually adopted a particular style and, if in the opinion of his coach, this is not to his advantage, it is far more difficult to break him of those habits and to steer him on to the right course.

Given a young player with natural ability and keenness to improve, what comes next? The answer is practice, hard and assiduous practice.

Cricket success, I repeat, depends to a great extent upon the individual. For instance, when the young player has achieved a certain amount of progress, it is not sufficient for him to rest on his newly won laurels. To retain them, to pass on to the next milestone, means more work, determined work—and that can only mean practice.

No man, not even the player who has gained County recognition, can sit back with the complacent outlook: "Well, I'm here and there's nothing else to be done." The player with that opinion would do himself and his future a favour if he packed up his cricket gear and never used it again. In any case, if he is too conceited and too headstrong to continue striving to retain the position he has gained, he will soon have no need for his cricket gear.

Complacency and cricket have nothing in common.

We are agreed that no player is perfect. Every cricketer, no matter whether he plays for his village team or for his County, has faults and weaknesses. But a complacent attitude will do nothing to rectify them. Constant and studious practice are the answer, the only answer.

Cricket, I will repeat, is a study that demands the complete co-operation and co-ordination of mind, limbs and muscles and this can only be attained from constant and detailed practice.

The player who is ambitious to do big things is never complacent, never satisfied that there is nothing left to learn. In cricket, as in all walks of life, it is the man who shows an appreciation of his faults and weaknesses, and spares no effort to remedy them, who is most likely to reap the highest reward for his endeavours.

IV

The Art of Batting

SO FAR we have discussed cricket in a general way, but now I want to deal in turn with the three specific phases of the game—batting, bowling and fielding. We will take them in that order—batting first.

A good worker in any sphere of life must have good tools, and that good worker, or one who wants to be good at his job, takes care of his tools. It is so in cricket, especially in batting, for nothing gives a player more confidence than to have faith in the tool he uses—in this case, his bat.

If it is possible I advise you all to have your own bat. It will repay you to spend time and thought in selecting a bat that suits you, one that is well balanced and with which you feel quite at home. You will never make runs easily and comfortably if you are using a bat that is too heavy or too unwieldly for you to handle.

I was always very particular about my own bats; they were my best friends on the cricket field. I used one particular willow throughout one whole season of County and representative matches, and although it was repaired several times before the summer's end, I scored over 2,500 runs with it. At the end of that memorable season that worn old bat had become so much a part of my cricketing self that I was really sorry to shelve it, but even bats won't go on for ever.

When you are fortunate enough to get a new bat, look after it. Don't hit the ball too hard with it at first. Play it in carefully for at least a week until the blade is

30

well weathered. During that first week, oil the face, as far as the splice, every day. When it is "played in" keep the face clean with sandpaper, and oil it occasionally to prevent it hardening and cracking.

Take every care of your bat if you want it to be a good friend, for a good bat is difficult to replace—and costly, too.

Having secured yourself a bat, what comes next? Grip and stance.

Young players are often curious to learn the correct way to hold the bat and how to stand at the wicket, but really there is no hard and fast rule governing these two points.

Be natural but firm in the way you hold your bat. Grip it as though you meant it, but make sure that the top of the handle touches the inside of your left wrist, so that the BACK of the hand FACES the bowler. That is absolutely vital, for any other grip will cause you to pull the ball when driving. Take a glance at the photograph following page 44.

Stance is another matter which must be left to the individual, but whatever pose you adopt, see that you stand in an easy and comfortable position at the crease. There must be nothing cramped about your stance or your batting will also be stiff and stolid. Stand evenly balanced on both feet, and make sure that your left shoulder is always facing the bowler. That is imperative if you are to play with a straight bat.

Actually the adoption of an easy, comfortable stance should not present many difficulties. Decide for yourself and then have enough confidence in your decision to stick to it.

That settles the choice of the bat, the grip and the

stance. Now will you allow me to offer a few general suggestions concerning the art of batting before I deal in detail with the main strokes?

The straight bat is the foundation of all good batting, and the only way to ensure the correct playing of strokes in front of the wicket is to keep the left elbow well up and the left shoulder well round. Thousands of times every season I am telling young players to keep the left elbow up. Drop it and you play across the ball and your intended stroke is ruined.

When I take a young batsman in hand, the first thing I try to teach him is when to play forward and when to play back, and again, when to play a forcing stroke and when to play a dead bat defensive shot. You can only become proficient in this fundamental of batting by studiously watching the ball leave the bowler's hand, for it is imperative to decide quickly what type of ball it is that is being sent down at you.

Immediately you detect the type of delivery—experience will soon teach you to pick out one from the other—make up your mind whether you will play a forcing or a defensive shot. It is often too late to arrive at a decision when the ball has pitched, and even if it is not too late, you are forced to make a hasty stroke, and hasty strokes are not good strokes. The quicker you "see" the ball, the more time you will have to position yourself for the right shot.

It cannot be stressed too strongly that the forward defensive shot MUST be mastered. I have found that it is a difficult shot for many young batsmen to play effectively, but as I always tell my lads, it is their best defence against good length bowling.

To make the shot confidently you play forward in the

Comfortable stance, evenly balanced on both feet.

Forward defensive stroke.

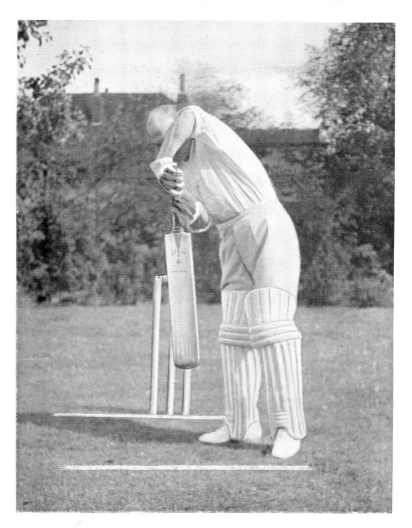

Backward defensive stroke.

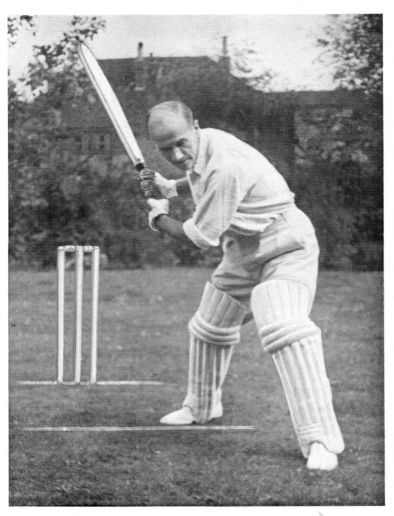

Position for on-driving a well-pitched-up ball near the leg stump.

Finish of a forward push stroke on a fast wicket to a good length ball on the legs.

Position for an off drive.

In position for a square cut.

Position for late cutting.

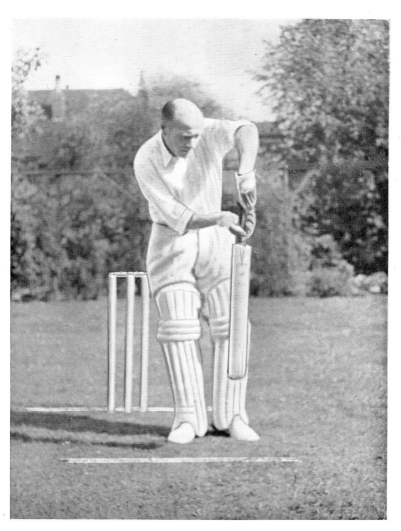

Playing a short-pitched ball near the leg stump to the on side.

Preparing to hit a slow ball outside the leg stump.

Position for short-arm hook shot.

A powerful drive through the covers.

ordinary way but, as opposed to the forward DRIVE, you loosen your grip and let the ball hit the dead bat.

Study the accompanying photograph and you will notice that when playing forward to a good length ball, it is only the left leg that moves. Note, too, that the bat does not move far from the left leg, thus leaving no gap through which the ball might spin.

When playing back to a short pitched ball on the wicket, both feet move half a step back towards the middle stump. Get your body well over the ball with your left elbow up, all your weight on the right foot with your left foot just touching the ground to keep you balanced. (See photograph.) Move quickly and be ready to force anything below stump high. Any ball that gets up higher than the stumps, play defensively.

Be very careful to keep your right foot glued to the ground when you play forward to a ball. If you over-reach, the right foot will be dragged from the crease. This is a common fault with young batsmen, and fatal, too, for if the ball beats the bat and the stumper is worth his place, the bails will be off in a twinkling.

My father stressed this point very forcibly when he was coaching me in my younger days. I soon realised the value of his advice and I was never guilty of reaching so far forward to a ball that I was thrown off my balance.

Throughout my career I was never stumped when playing a forward shot. I am not inferring that I was NEVER stumped. I was dismissed in that way on several occasions, but only when I had run down the pitch to hit out at a slow bowler, after I had collected a big score.

My early games with Essex taught me plenty about the art of batting, and one of the most important of those lessons was that it was no disgrace to take time to play myself in when I took my place at the wickets.

Use the first few overs of your innings to get your eye in. Get a good sight of the ball. Play it carefully without thinking about runs. Try to measure up the strength of the bowling and the pace of the pitch. Remember what I said in an earlier chapter about getting acclimatised to the middle before you think about moving the score along.

Some players are inclined to get flustered when they cannot score freely early on in their innings. Why be so perturbed? My advice is—Take your time. Get a feel of the ball. Once your eye is in the ball will begin to look bigger and you can go for the runs. Don't forget, the longer you stay at the wickets, the easier you will find run-getting.

You should never become unduly worried if the bowlers are on top and attacking so consistently that scoring is slow and difficult. In such circumstances it is just a matter of waiting until the bowlers begin to tire. If you are anything of a batsman you should be able to make up lost time when the bowling slackens.

I saw a young batsman last season who was playing perfect defensive cricket in one particular match against some excellent bowling. He was playing exactly the right game in the circumstances, but suddenly he began to hit out, and two balls later he was bowled.

When he returned to the pavilion he apologised for his action.

"I got tired of playing ball after ball defensively," he said. "I lost my patience and thought I should be able to knock the bowler off his length . . ."

"But it didn't turn out like that, did it?" I interposed.

No, it doesn't pay to get flustered at the wickets. If you play the right game it will be the bowlers who will crack first.

I recall very vividly a match against Somerset at Leyton. Their swing bowlers had us pegged down. My Essex partner and I refused to be lured into making a false move and we were at the wickets for quite a long time without scoring, simply because the bowling was so good that it would have been asking for trouble to open up at that stage.

The spectators grew restless at our apparent lack of action, but still we played the bowlers at their own game. Our opening wickets had fallen cheaply and although I naturally would rather have had a go at the bowling, I was not keen to give the Somerset attackers another cheap victim. In any case, to have done so would have been bad team work.

Maiden followed maiden. Still we played defensively, and then, eventually, down came one or two loose balls. These were promptly punished, and it was not so long before my partner and I began to make up for that period of inactivity.

I collared the later bowling to such good purpose that I had scored 236 before I was out. Had I not been content to wait for the right moment to attack the Somerset bowling, the result might have been very different.

If you have the patience to bide your time, you can rest assured that the runs will come—all in good time.

Should you be faced with a similar position to that I have just described, remember that you are not playing entirely for yourself. Cricket is a team game and you are a member of that team, and a man in the middle is worth two in the pavilion.

By all means make the most of your chances, while you are at the wicket, but take no unnecessary risks. Concentration is one of the fundamentals in the mental make-up of the first-class batsman. Never relax for a moment, because it is in that unwary moment that you will be beaten,

Don Bradman is one of the world's greatest batsmen, and certainly the most heartbreaking man to bowl against. I speak from experience. The great little Australian captain has amazing powers of concentration. He is always watching every ball right on to his bat, and even when he has compiled a big score, he is ever on the alert for any new guile or ruse attempted by the hard-worked bowlers. It is true to say that Bradman's concentration is as great after he has scored 300 as it was when he was building up the first 50 of his mammoth scores. What a model for young batsmen to follow.

The really sound batsman never takes a deliberate risk. That is, he does nothing that will endanger his wicket.

I recall an occasion when my enthusiasm for runs caused me to take a risk that ended in my swift return to the pavilion. We were playing at Gloucester and my own score had reached 99 when I foolishly chased a wide ball on the off-side.

I should have left it alone but for once I forgot all the advice I had been given as a lad. I managed to reach out and touch that ball, but it shot off the edge of the blade and I was caught behind the wicket.

One foolish, needless risk meant that I not only missed my century, but I threw away my wicket when the side was still in need of runs—and that was bad teamwork.

Only last summer I was guilty of a bad error of

judgment. Playing at Slough in a Minor Counties game against Staffordshire, I had a good chance to save the game for Bucks. In my urgent eagerness, I called for a quick single. It was a foolish call, one that I should never have made after all my years in cricket, and I had only myself to blame when I was smartly run out, just at a most vital stage of the game.

I have told you that the good batsman never takes a risk, but the incidents I have just recalled were two occasions when I forgot that very sound advice, and although they are not to my credit, the relating of them should provide a lesson for you all and help to emphasise the value of my contention.

No batsman can be blamed if he is dismissed when making an effort to force the pace when the side is in need of quick runs, but it is my experience that too many good wickets are wasted, usually through momentary relaxing of concentration, or because of over-confidence.

Many teams have lost a match by a mere few runs. Often in such cases the result might have been so different but for one batsman, his eye in and the runs coming freely, taking a risk—"having a bang," for instance, and presenting his wicket to the opposing side.

There is an invigorating feeling about using the long handle and few batsmen can resist the temptation when the occasion presents itself. Nothing is more pleasing to player and spectator alike than to see the ball flying high and wide, but there is always a risk in that style of play if the bowler is skilful enough to make you play to his field.

Do not misunderstand me. I should be the last person to advocate "stick-in-the-mud" batting, but runs can be scored quickly and the cricket can be made intensely interesting by batsmen who keep the ball on the carpet. Four well-timed, well-placed singles, the result of correct stroke play, are better than a mighty hit into the air which might result in a catch. There is ever that risk, and the good batsman, as I have said, does not take risks. If I may be permitted to misquote the old adage: A run on the ground is worth two in the air.

Before we leave batting risks, I want to advise batsmen not to chase balls outside the off stump, especially during the early overs of an innings. By all means make use of such balls by watching them off the pitch: they are an invaluable help towards gauging the pace of the wicket, but if you go nibbling at good length balls outside the off stump you are asking for trouble.

By the way, if you intend allowing a ball outside the off stump to go through to the keeper, don't take any chances with it. Step across your wicket so that your legs are OUTSIDE the off stump, thus covering your wicket should the ball break back, and yet not run any danger of being given out l.b.w.

Now we come to another important phase of batting—running between the wickets. This, actually, is an art in itself, an art that must be studied and developed until it nears perfection, for matches are won and lost by good or bad running.

Confidence, both in your own judgment and in the quick decisions of your partner, is the essence of success in running, for remember, although one of the two men at the wickets actually hits the ball, it takes both of them, working in close harmony, to complete each run.

There must be co-operation then, so if it is your call then shout smartly, either "Come one!" or "No, wait!" Call what you like, of course, so long as you call something after EACH forcing shot, and when you run, keep your eye on the ball. If you feel there is a second run, then let your partner know your intentions as you cross in mid-wicket.

You may hit the ball behind your wicket and thus lose sight of it. Never mind, put your faith in your partner's call and back him up. Whatever you do, don't stand hesitant. If, for any reason, however, you feel that to act on your partner's call and run would be too dangerous, then don't be frightened to tell your partner so and send him back. But don't dither and hesitate. Call quickly, while there is still ample time for him to get back to his crease.

He who hesitates, when a run is called for, is lost.

Always run the first run as though you meant it, for you should ever be on the look out for a second, prepared for a fielder to fumble his pick-up. In any case, by giving the field the impression that you intend to go for two, you often bustle fielders into fumbling or into hasty and inaccurate throwing in.

There is more in successful running than most batsmen realise. Here's another point. The two men at the wickets should avoid running too close together, but should keep well clear of one another, on opposite sides of the pitch to prevent any possibility of a collision in mid-wicket. I have seen this happen quite often, even in County cricket, and while the batsmen are sorting themselves out of a tangle, which is entirely of their own making, one of them finds himself run out. You may think this is a small point, but the player who watches the small points is the one who will achieve big success.

Learn to back up your partner, for good backing up turns many a single into a two. Always be ready for that quick dash down the pitch, but here I must issue another word of warning. If you are the non-striker, don't be TOO eager to back-up, or perhaps I should say, don't back up too far.

Another of my own personal memories will explain what I mean.

Some years ago, playing for Essex against Derbyshire, I had scored 49. Laurie Eastman, at the other end, was attacking the bowling in his inimitable way and I was backing up, well out of my crease, when he hit a ball straight down the pitch. I started to run—and I didn't stop until I reached the pavilion!

You see the ball passed me, struck the bowler's foot and rebounded on to the wicket I had just left. I was yards out of my crease: in fact, I was out in more ways than one.

Back up by all means, you'd be a bad batsman and a poor partner if you didn't, but don't lift your bat from the crease until you feel that it is safe to start your run.

Always run for a lofted ball, too. No matter if it looks as though a fielder has been presented with a "dolly" catch, run. He may drop it. (Fielders have been known to drop catches, you know.)

Just one further point. A batsman should never race down the pitch for his first run at such an uncontrolled speed that he cannot stop and turn quickly when he reaches the other wicket. His partner turns for a second —or for an overthrow, maybe—but the run cannot be accepted because one of the two partners is not in a position to back up.

This is often caused by bad spiking or lack of spikes in the boots. So many batsmen are run out through slipping at a vital moment because their boots are inefficiently spiked. Watch that point. See that your boots are properly spiked before you step out on to the field.

Do concentrate on your running. Back up, watch points, and don't be afraid to call to your partner, and you'll be surprised at the extra runs you score.

Every run counts—yes, EVERY run, so try not to waste your scoring chances. Take all the runs that are there for the taking, for neglected runs often make a difference to the result of the game.

On that point memory recalls an occasion in my own career when I had very good reason for regretting the slow running response from my partners earlier in this particular innings.

It was in a match against Middlesex at Clacton. When the fifth Essex wicket fell, my own score stood at 99. But G. O. Allen, the England fast bowler, skittled our last five batsmen in such rapid succession that I did not receive another ball, and the end came with my total still 99 not out.

Had it not been for some rather lethargic running between the wickets during the early part of that innings —singles not accepted; certain twos that produced only singles—I might have passed my hundred long before "Gubby" Allen set about the tail-enders.

By the way, have you ever considered how much runs are worth? Actually, you know, figures are comparative. The value of an individual innings is not in the NUMBER of runs scored but in the conditions in which they are scored. Fifty runs collected in a backs-to-the-wall struggle, or on a difficult wicket, are often worth far more to your side than a hundred scored on an easy-paced wicket when the position is not so desperate and the opposition not so keen.

I remember vividly the day when I was awarded my County cap. It was a match against Yorkshire, at Leyton, in 1923. After heavy rain the wicket was a beast, a real "sticky dog." Every run had to be forced and boundaries —even couples—were at a premium owing to the slowness of the outfield. However, in a long and painstaking innings I managed to score 60 before I was caught in trying a big hit.

In the pavilion afterwards, Johnnie Douglas, our skipper, congratulated me.

"Jack," he said, "you'll never play a better innings. That sixty was worth a hundred on any ordinary wicket. Here's your County cap—you've earned it."

Although I scored well over 27,000 runs in first-class cricket, I shall always remember that knock against Yorkshire, the innings that brought me my blue Essex County cap, still one of my most treasured possessions.

Batsmen should take every opportunity of practising on sticky wickets. The majority of cricketers should manage to hit up even a few runs on a hard, true pitch, but it is vastly different when the "middle" is playing tricks following rain. It is then that a batsman can prove his mettle.

One or two other small, but important, "do's" and "dont's."

Don't stay in the pavilion after you have padded up. Sit out in the strong light and get your eyes attuned to it. You won't have time when you get to the wickets and the bowlers are after your blood.

Don't worry too much about the stumps behind you. Defend them by all means, but concentrate all your attention on the ball in front of you, and if your timing is right and you get the ball in the middle of the bat, you will not need to concern yourself about the stumps.

Take every precaution when you are newly arrived at the crease, but once you feel you are seeing the ball, then keep looking for runs. Always be ready to punish the loose ball and when you hear the umpire call "No ball!" let it have the stick. Remember, you cannot be bowled or caught off a no-ball.

One final word. When I talk about "punishing" a ball I am not suggesting that brute force alone will score runs. As a matter of fact, the good batsman never resorts to slogging—slogging, that is, as opposed to good solid hitting or driving. They are poles apart.

A hit is a drive or a stroke executed with deliberate purpose, the result of the co-ordination of eye, wrist and footwork. Slogging, on the other hand, is wild smiting of the ball, usually with a cross-bat, with which the batsman has little command of direction.

The good batsman, by means of accurate stroke play, can score as fast as the unorthodox hitter, but without running so much risk.

Let me see stroke play every time, for stroke play is batsmanship.

V

Have You ever hit a Hundred?

THE STRAIGHT bat is the foundation of sound batting. That has been stated before but it bears repetition. The straight bat is the basis of all the main strokes in the batsman's repertoire, as you will realise when I introduce you to some of them.

First, the drive, which is the most widely executed stroke, for nearly all the aggressive shots in front of the wicket can be termed drives.

There are three orthodox drives—the ON, the OFF, and the STRAIGHT—and they do not differ a great deal, except in the direction in which the ball is played. Footwork is vital to the success of all these strokes. In each case, the left leg moves forward, the foot moving out to the pitch of the ball.

The accompanying photographs should serve to illustrate the foot and body action for the off and on drives. Note that the weight of the body is thrown forward on to the left leg, with the bat following straight through in a natural swing.

There is really little advice which can be given about the off drive, for it is what is known as a "natural" shot. But the on-drive, hit wide of mid-on from a ball pitched well up on the legs, often presents difficulty to young players, but once it is mastered it can prove a most useful and profitable run-getting shot.

As a young player I was dismissed several times because of an inability to make the on-drive with any confidence. Coaching and practice enabled me to master the shot, however, and in later years I scored hundreds of runs with it.

The important point to remember when making this stroke is to put the left foot outside the ball and not straight at it, so that there is room for the bat to STRIKE the ball.

One of the most gratifying of all shots is the one you use when you jump out to drive the really slow bowler. Once you are set and there is a good score on the board, there is nothing against attacking the bowling in this way, but let me warn you, however, not to overdo this form of attack.

When you jump out to a ball, make sure that you get to the pitch of the ball, and keep your head well down. Don't give the bowler any idea of your intentions as he delivers the ball; otherwise, if he is a master of his art, he may quickly change his pace and direction and your stroke will be ruined before it is made.

Quickness of eye and fleet footwork are essential if you are to use these attacking tactics effectively, because if you make just one mistake you will almost certainly have lost your wicket, for once you have jumped down the pitch your chance of a swift recovery to your crease is very slim. So jump out by all means, when the occasion presents itself and the circumstances are right, but be sure of yourself.

Two of the most delightful and most graceful strokes in the whole batting curriculum are the cuts—late and square. They differ very considerably, of course, although both are used for dealing with short-pitched balls on the off, and both depend on a quick eye and sure footwork for their successful accomplishment.

For the square cut, that sends the ball past point, the

right leg is moved across the wicket, with the right toe facing point, as you will see from the accompanying photograph. With the late cut, so called because the bat does not connect until the ball is practically level with the wicket, or even passing it, the right leg moves to a position OUTSIDE the off stump, with the right toe facing second slip, before actual contact is made. Don't let that puzzle you; just glance at the photograph of the stroke and you should see clearly what I mean.

In both forms of cut, however, the face of the bat must come down well on top of the ball so that the ball strikes the ground before it speeds away past the fielders. If you cut a ball with the face of the bat turned even slightly upward, then the blame will be entirely your own if third slip or gully gratefully snaps up a catch.

To learn more about the cut, which is a wonderful shot if played correctly, I would suggest that you try to watch one of the prominent County or Test batsmen in action, men like Denis Compton and Len Hutton, for example. They are among the best of the modern exponents of the cut, but the most artistic and accurate cutter of a ball I ever saw was Andy Sandham, the little Surrey opening batsman. Andy's timing of a ball on the off, especially when he was employing the late cut, was well nigh uncanny.

I often wish I could have watched my uncle, Bob Carpenter, batting, for old cricketers consider him to be the finest player of the late cut the game has ever known. From another very old Essex cricketer I learned that bowlers were often forced to bring up extra slips in an effort to prevent Uncle Bob scoring with his pet stroke, the late cut. That in itself, proves that he must have been an expert at that fine stroke.

Timing is another batting fundamental, as you will realise, but in no phase of run-getting is it more essential than in strokes on the leg side. Many of these are executed from fast deliveries, and, in consequence, split second timing is vital.

Watch out, though, and make certain that the ball will miss the leg peg, before you attempt a leg stroke. Actually, it is not necessary to hit fast bowling on the leg. A quick movement of the feet towards the stumps, a touch of the bat, and the ball should go glancing down to fine leg. It is just a matter of accurate timing and a flick of the wrist. Off slower deliveries, however, you must turn sharply and strike hard.

We have now dealt with drives, cuts and leg strokes, and come next to the hook. Now this stroke is so difficult to execute efficiently and without risk, that I do not advise its use by young batsmen with limited experience.

Many a youthful run-getter has regretted attempting to hook a high, bumping ball. I learned a very severe lesson in my second County match. It was against Middlesex at Leyton, and I had 25 on the board when I faced Jack Durston, the tall fast bowler.

Down came one of Jack's expresses. Having hooked several of his previous deliveries, I intended to repeat the stroke, but this particular ball was slightly faster than the previous ones. I attempted a hook, but the pace off the pitch deceived me. Instead of connecting with the middle of the bat, the ball hit the splice and I was caught at short leg. It would have been far better to have played an ordinary backward defensive shot.

Although the hook shot is one of the most difficult of all strokes, it can be learned and developed if your eye is good enough. Following the dismissal of which I have

47

just told you, I spent weeks practising the hook, and later scored many runs with the stroke. So did my old friend Patsy Hendren, who seemed to revel in bowling that "got up around his ears."

Just a word on the correct way to hook a ball. It will help you to appreciate and understand the accompanying photograph of the hook shot.

For a short pitched ball on the wicket, move across quickly to the off, so that you get your head to the right side of the line of the ball. Watch the ball closely and then sweep the bat round. If you fail to move your head quickly enough and you miss hitting the ball, then the ball is likely to hit you, or you will mistime it and will probably be caught.

You may be one of the small band of cricketers who are natural hookers; in other words you may find no difficulty in dealing with short pitched balls in this way. If you are, then don't let me stop you. But if you cannot hook with natural ease, then don't try. Play an ordinary backward defensive shot to anything that is short pitched or bumped at you, for remember that the ball must be pitched VERY short, somewhere about halfway, to give you ample time to move into position for an effective hook shot.

Be careful, however. Never attempt to hook early on in your innings before your eye is in; and if the ball is bumped too high, that is, more than head high, on no account attempt to touch it. Leave it alone.

Before we leave stroke play, let me emphasise again the need to be ever on the alert when you are at the crease. Make up your mind quickly about the stroke you are going to play, and don't try to force a ball if you find that you have been mistaken in your original decision.

Take no chances. Change your intended stroke into a defensive forward or half-cock stroke.

Remember, too, that in all strokes the bat should be swinging slowly back towards the stumps from the blockhole as the ball is delivered, ready to come down on it as soon as it pitches. In other words, do not wait until the ball is right on to your bat before you start your stroke.

It might be advisable now to discuss the essentials needed for the various positions in the batting order, for too little thought is given to the value of team work in batting. It is vital to success.

The opening pair are, perhaps, the most important members of the batting side, for they, more than any of their comrades, must be specialists and partners in every respect. The opening batsmen are called upon to face the attack when the bowlers are fresh and can make full use of the shine on the ball to swing their deliveries.

It behoves the opening batsmen, therefore, to play steadily and safely, to take the shine off the ball with as little delay as possible and the initial sting out of the bowlers, while waiting for the right ball to hit. No chances can be taken, for it is up to the openers to give the side a good start, to pave the way for the following batsmen.

Nothing gives the later batsmen more confidence than to know that there is a good score on the board when their turn comes to walk out to the wickets. On the other hand, the early dismissal of the opening pair can cause the rout of the whole side. I've seen it happen so often, and when a rot sets in, it is not easy to arrest it.

During my years in first-class cricket I saw some wonderful opening pairs in action. I was called upon to bowl against many of them, and oft-times I have wished for some miracle to happen that would part them.

I have very vivid recollections of those Yorkshire "twins," Herbert Sutcliffe and Percy Holmes, who, in 1932 registered a record first wicket stand of 555 against Essex at Leyton. Who could forget that marvellous exploit? I sent down twenty-three overs during their brilliant partnership and although my bowling was well and truly hit all round the Essex ground, I could not but admire the consummate skill and patience of the inseparable Yorkshire pair.

Apart from their huge score, however, there was nothing unusual or extraordinary about the batting of Herbert and Percy in that great performance. Throughout the whole of their long innings which lasted 7 hours and 25 minutes, they played their normal game, scoring steadily all the time, but never relaxing their concentration and never taking the slightest risk. It was their mental attitude and their lack of nerves as they approached the old record (set up incidentally by Yorkshiremen, Brown and Tunnicliffe in 1898) that made most impression upon me. They were imperturbable. To them it was just another innings, one of hundreds they had played together.

That is the only way to approach any innings and for that reason I wish all young cricketers could have seen that record opening partnership. It was certainly one of the most immaculate I ever saw, but then Sutcliffe and Holmes were born partners and ideal openers, because not only was each a brilliant batsman in his own right, but both possessed the temperament which is so necessary to the outstanding first wicket pair.

Cricket sparkled with good opening batsmen in my playing days, but on reflection I feel that I must vote for Hobbs and Sandham as the most accomplished first wicket PAIR I ever met on the field of play, Jack Hobbs was the complete master of all occasions, with Andy Sandham his very able and capable assistant, and had not Sutcliffe been so outstanding a run-getter and so imperturbable in temperament in Test cricket, it is more than likely that "Sandy" would have partnered his Surrey colleague in many England sides, for they played together so long that their combination became almost instinctive.

In modern cricket there are a number of first-class individual first wicket men—Hutton, Washbrook, Barnett, Fletcher (Surrey), Robertson and others—but I have yet to see an opening PAIR to equal that completeness of co-ordination and co-operation at the wickets displayed by Sutcliffe and Holmes, or Hobbs and Sandham, or Sutcliffe and Hobbs in Test matches.

That was by the way, so let us return to the subject and discuss other batsmen who are necessary to the all-round success of a side.

First wicket down should be a sound batsman with all the shots, a profound enthusiast for his onerous job, with much of the temperament of the opening pair, for he may be called upon to replace one of the openers who has been dismissed cheaply. Because of this he must be so equipped that he is prepared to play the waiting game against the fast bowlers until the shine is off the ball. That was my job during most of my years with Essex and I would not have changed it for any other.

I suggest that Bill Edrich is the finest modern example of the tiptop No. 3 batsman, for here is a man who can adapt his batting to the changing state of the game, as he has proved so often, and when the time is ripe, he does not mind "having a go."

Nos. 4 and 5—the former particularly—are the hammer-heads of the batting, the men on whom the side can rely to get on with the scoring when the initial sting is out of the bowling. Their job is to push the score along at a goodly pace.

You should know the style of man needed for this specialised job, Patsy Hendren, Maurice Leyland, and Walter Hammond, all of the "old school," and Denis Compton of the present generation of Test players. Denis Compton—what a batsman, what a headache to the bowlers, and what a heartache to the fielders.

In my ideal batting side I also like to see a few reliable all-rounders to fill the positions from No. 6 onwards, each capable of collecting runs when the position demands. All-rounders are most valuable when the early and middle batsmen have failed.

All-rounders can make a side. The Yorkshire eleven of pre-war years who, season after season topped the County Championship, had its star batsmen, but in my opinion its success lay in its seasoning of experienced all-rounders who made it possible for Yorkshire to claim that they had no tail.

Essex is another good example. During my many seasons with them we had, apart from myself, Morris Nichols, who seldom missed achieving the cricketer's "double"; Laurie Eastman; Johnnie Douglas (another of cricket's "1,000 and 100" experts); Peter Smith and his cousin Ray Smith, (both of whom secured the "double" for the first time in their careers last season). Essex have a reputation for all-rounders and a position has always been found in the County eleven for young players who reveal themselves qualified to bat AND bowl.

Cricket would be lost without its all-rounders and it is

always a pleasure to find a lad who is anxious to make himself proficient as batsman and bowler, although I am not suggesting that a young cricketer should neglect any outstanding natural aptitude he may possess in one particular phase of the game in an effort to try to master both batting AND bowling. You know the old saying about "Jack of all trades and master of none . . ." In cricket, however, it all depends upon the individual whether this is true or not.

There is something satisfying about being an all-rounder. Possessing proficiency to some degree at both batting and bowling means that, should you fail at one, you have the chance to retrieve your failure at the other. Second chances are always welcome.

There is a more important factor even than that, however. My own practical experience and knowledge of bowling materially helped my batting and gave me more confidence to face the bowling, especially the spin stuff, which was my own pet style. To have practical knowledge of the other chap's job helps a cricketer, whether he be batsman or bowler, to be better equipped mentally.

So if you feel that you are strong enough and keen enough to have a go at mastering the arts of batting AND bowling, by all means do so. If you succeed, your value to your side will be enhanced. The all-rounder derives more enjoyment from his cricket and more satisfaction from the fact that he is always in the game, playing an active part whether his team are batting or in the field.

No discussion on batting would be complete without some mention of the scoring of a century.

A young college batsman came up to me on one occasion and said:

"Mr. O'Connor, as you know I'm usually good for a

few runs and I've hit up several fifties and sixties, but I cannot seem to get my hundred. What is wrong with my play?"

"There's nothing wrong with your actual play," I answered, for I knew this lad's capabilities at the wickets. "You lack sufficient concentration, that is all. You play yourself in and, with correct stroke play, you find the runs beginning to flow easily from your bat; but then you become over-confident and your concentration relaxes. You make one false stroke, or one mis-stroke, and you are out."

I have encountered it so often. In the summer of 1926, before I had become complete master of my century temperament, I scored 1,402 runs in first-class games, and yet I did not register one individual hundred. In 14 innings I collected scores of 50 or over, my highest being 84. But a hundred—no, I just could not reach three figures.

Perseverance and patience enabled me to pass through that phase and in later years I collected plenty of hundreds, but it was an experience that taught me a lesson, and I never objected to learning.

But concerning this business of scoring a century, really, you know, if a fellow can stay at the crease long enough to reach 25, there should be no reason why he should not remain to score a hundred—provided, of course, that he has the requisite ability, takes no needless risks and can maintain his concentration and care over his strokes without tiring. All that and the luck being in his favour, of course.

It is easy to theorise. It is a far different matter when you are out in the centre with eleven other fellows all striving to send you back to the pavilion, but there is no reason why you should not know what I consider the best prescription for the scoring of a century.

My own maiden hundred in County cricket taught me a great deal that was to prove useful to my future. It was at Northampton in my third County game. I was slow in starting on a good wicket, but I was acting on the advice of my coaches, who had told me to get acclimatised. Remember what I told you about that?

Gradually, as I settled down and became more at ease, I had the feeling that this was to be my day. It was up to me to make the most of it.

I had scored centuries before, in lower grades of cricket, but I imagined that the collecting of a hundred in a County game would be a similar experience. I was wrong. It proved quite different from anything that had gone before.

As I said in a previous chapter, one of my deepest impressions when I took my place in the senior game was the very much keener fielding, compared with what I had encountered in the minor ranks, and the skill with which captains and bowlers changed their field in an effort to lay traps for unwary batsmen. In the face of such circumstances, I quickly realised that if I was to reach my first hundred in that match at Northampton, I should need to concentrate more than ever before.

The skipper tried all his bowlers in an effort to lure me into mistakes. He even called upon Fanny Walden, the famous little Tottenham Hotspur footballer, to send down some of his exceedingly slow deliveries, hoping to tempt me to hit out—and get out.

I refused to be drawn and went on steadily and surely to a score of 102 not out.

It was a memorable milestone in my life and naturally

I felt pleased with myself, but I was then still only a very young and comparatively inexperienced cricketer, and I knew that one century didn't make me famous.

That maiden century, however, did teach me the need for constant care and concentration over every ball and every shot, although I was rather surprised that I felt no nerves during that century innings, not even when I reached the oft mis-named "nervous nineties." I remember that I forgot everything else but the job on hand and treated every ball with all the respect it deserved.

If you will allow me to deviate for a moment, I should like to tell you of the century that gave me most satisfaction. It is not easy to do this, for I scored 73 individual hundreds in County cricket, including one such innings against each of the other Counties.

On reflection I think I shall plump for the century against Hampshire at Leyton some years back. If it wasn't my best innings from the point of view of classic style, at least it is considered to be the most valuable I ever hit for Essex.

In the fourth innings, on a pig of a wicket, we needed 183 to win the match. I had been dismissed for a duck in the first innings and before we batted for the last time I heard Lord Tennyson, the Hampshire skipper, tell some of his team that they should be able to dismiss us quickly and allow themselves plenty of time to catch the early train back to Southampton.

In view of the state of the wicket, it certainly looked odds on an easy and swift victory for Hampshire, but in cricket, as in all sports, certainties have a strange habit of coming unstuck. This one did.

The Essex run-getters made a bad start and the first six wickets went down for only 60 runs, but I managed to stay, battling almost alone against the wiles of those two grand bowlers Kennedy and Newman. If ever I needed patience and concentration I did that afternoon, for I felt that the result of the match depended upon me and me alone.

To cut a long story short, eventually we scored the winning hit and I had collected 111 of the 183 runs needed for victory. (No, the Hampshire players did NOT catch their early train home!)

Actually, you know, nothing extraordinary is needed to reach a hundred with the bat. Just play your normal game, don't get flustered and don't let the scoreboard worry you. The longer you remain in the middle, the easier you should find run-getting, and the last ten runs between ninety and a hundred should present no greater difficulties than the earlier runs. It all depends upon the mental outlook of the individual.

During your innings you may give a chance to the field that is not accepted. All of us have had that experience, but some players I have known have allowed such a "miss" to unnerve them and they have tried to be even more careful with their next shots. The result often has been over-caution—and dismissal.

If you are missed, no matter in what way, say to yourself: "Lucky fellow. You've been given a let-off so make the most of it."

That is the only way to view an experience of that nature.

Herbert Sutcliffe was a master at it. With his stoical Yorkshire calm he would continue his masterful batting following one of those fortunate incidents that come to all cricketers, as though nothing untoward had happened. Oft-times I have seen him go on to score a century after being missed early on in his innings.

E

It is all a matter of temperament, for I will repeat, the mental outlook plays a very great part in cricket. It certainly can have a great bearing upon the success or failure of a batsman.

Nerves have sent many a batsman back to the pavilion before he has had a chance to settle down. Of course, this doesn't mean that there is something wrong with you if you feel strung up before you take guard. This is a very human failing. I have known cricketers of many years' experience who went pale at the thought of facing an innings; others who have been unable to buckle on their own pads.

If the fellow suffering from nerves allows his play to be affected to any degree, or if his nerves force him to make a rash or hasty stroke when he reaches the wicket, more often than not he finds himself back in the pavilion.

Once you survive the first over, everything seems to be all right. As soon as you have played a ball or two you are sure to feel better. Nerves are natural, but the individual's own strength of will can do much to dispel them quickly.

Try to tell yourself what I always told myself when I felt a trifle tremulous because of the importance, maybe, of the match in which I was batting: "They can only bowl one ball at me at a time." So play every ball on its merits.

The bowler has the ball; you have the bat. The next step is up to you and you only. If you can keep your nerves under control for the first few balls, your confidence will quickly return. But let your nerves get the better of you and you won't be at the wickets long enough to do anything at all—except walk back to the pavilion.

Temperament—yes, it plays such a big part in all cricket.

Don't, for instance, become disconsolate if you are sent back because of a mistaken decision of an umpire, or at least a decision which you feel should never have been given against you. Remember that umpires are only human—and who hasn't made a mistake?

I recall an occasion when I was given out, on appeal, for a catch behind the stumps, and yet I knew that I had not touched the ball. I was young at the time and naturally felt a trifle discouraged and a little peeved. In the very next match, however, I should have been out off my first ball. I put my leg in front of one that should have broken to the off, but which came straight through. The bowler appealed loudly, but, to my amazement, the umpire refused the appeal. I took advantage of that lucky let-off to score a century.

Cricket is like that; you can never guarantee what fortune has in store for you. The mistaken decision against you one day may be in your favour on the next occasion.

Success, or the lack of it, often follows the same course. Out of luck and out of form one day may quite easily become in luck and bang in form the next. That is, of course, if your mental outlook is right. But if you allow a run of misfortune or "mis-form", through whatever cause, to affect your play, you will be lucky if you do not stay down.

Put every experience as a batsman in its right perspective. Don't get unduly discouraged, but, on the contrary, do not let it be said that you have suddenly outgrown the size of your cap. Swollen head never took a cricketer to the top. In any case, many a batsman has scored a century one day—only to collect a large blob on the scorebook in his very next innings.

VI

Take Care and You'll Take Wickets!

NOW THEN, all you bowlers and would-be wicket-takers, let us discuss your particular section of the game; the most important, too, in my estimation, for without bowling there could be no batting.

You may not agree with me, but it is my considered opinion that it is harder to become a good bowler than a good batsman. The mastery of the bowling arts needs more concentrated study. There are good reasons for that contention.

On average wickets the batsmen with few strokes and a limited knowledge of the finer points of batting, can usually manage to scrape up a few runs, but the bowler with limited ability and experience is not likely to take many wickets, not with any real consistency at least, and certainly not without his bowling analysis reaching astronomical proportions.

The bowling arts are not quickly or easily mastered—nor, for that matter, can efficient batting be developed overnight—but to become a really accurate bowler necessitates hard work and plenty of it, too. If the young cricketer hasn't the capacity for really tiring, heart-breaking spells of strenuous work, then he may as well forget his ambition to become a bowler.

For this, many qualities are necessary, and not the least important of these is the possession of the right mental outlook. This is imperative, for it plays such a prominent part in the bowler's development.

Call it temperament if you prefer it—temperament,

not temper, for the bowler who loses his temper, or becomes ruffled when he is harshly treated by hard-hitting batsmen, loses everything and gains little but the scorn of the batsmen opposed to him. The chap with the bat shows no sympathy with the fellow who cannot take punishment.

If you hope to be a successful bowler you'll need confidence, courage and a big heart, for you'll be called upon to take plenty of hard knocks. Your bowling will be hit and hit mighty hard at times, for batsmen are no respecters of bowlers, and you cannot expect lenient treatment, especially on good wickets.

I remember my father telling me when I was just a lad and feeling a little disconsolate after being hit all over the field:

"Don't lose your head, lad. The bowler who was never clouted never took a wicket. Keep pegging away at them."

I tried not to forget this when I ascended into the County game. In an early match with Essex it seemed that the opposing batsmen had a grudge against me, for they appeared to take a delight in clouting me to the four winds. Naturally I felt a trifle upset at their treatment, but I kept pegging away at them.

It was then that I was given another word of advice that was to help me in later years. One of the older Essex professionals spoke to me as we changed over. "Pitch them slightly to the off," he said. "Make the batsmen reach for the ball—but don't lose your length."

I acted on the suggestion, and although more runs came it was not long before one of the batsmen reached out to drive a ball on the off-side, only to snick it and be snapped up in the slips.

It does you no good to become disheartened when the

61

fellow with the bat is knocking your bowling to ribbons. Some batsmen will deliberately—but quite fairly, mind you—try to hit out at the early deliveries of a young bowler in an effort to knock him off his length and upset his temperament, so that he will resort to sending down loose stuff in his desperation and desire to cut down the scoring.

It is in such circumstances that the bowler who is endeavouring to make his mark can prove himself and show that he has the heart and the mental capacity that helps to make the really good bowler. If he gives way to his anxiety, he will be punished harder than ever.

Things will not always go right, you know. I have experienced days when I have bowled really well, beating the bat time after time and getting right on top of the batsmen, but without taking any wickets. An experience of that sort is inclined to rattle some bowlers and cause despondency, but it is just one of those things that happen to all cricketers and must be viewed philosophically.

But then there is the reverse experience, when you bowl poorly and feel that you are right off form—and yet you get wickets.

That happened to me at Worcester in 1925. Before lunch on the first day the early Worcester batsmen got right on top. The regular Essex bowlers could do little against them and the Worcester score stood at something like 100 for no wickets when Johnnie Douglas slung me the ball.

"See what you can do with your spinners, Jack," he said.

My first delivery was an atrocious ball, a long hop. Now most batsmen know how to treat a long hop and H. K. Foster was too good a cricketer to miss such a

Heaven-sent opportunity. He slammed it away towards square leg—and was caught.

My second ball, another bad one, was a full toss. The batsman who had just come in was M. K. Foster, brother of H. K. He mistimed it and hit it straight back to me —caught and bowled.

In came Gilbert Ashton, one of the famous Essex cricketing family, and down went my third ball, another long hop, for it seemed impossible for me to find a length. Yes, another long hop—but to my amazement Gilbert Ashton hit it straight into short leg's hands.

Three wickets in three balls, a hat-trick, and yet I had sent down three really bad balls, each of which should have been cracked for four.

You should have heard the comments of my Essex colleagues. They were not very complimentary—in a joking way, of course, for they were as pleased as I was to see those three wickets fall so cheaply.

It was just the luck of the game. I am not suggesting however, that you deliberately bowl bad balls in the hope of taking wickets when things are not going well for your side. I only recalled that incident to illustrate my point that it isn't always the fellow who is bowling on top of his form who will get the wickets. This is usually the case, but not always.

So don't be disheartened if you bowl well without success. Your day will come if you can see every experience in its right perspective, and take your big chance when it presents itself.

No bowler achieves success without practice, and by practice I do not mean anything haphazard but hard, concentrated work. Net practice is invaluable to the bowler, but let me impress upon you, as it was always stressed to me, that you bowl at the nets with the same whole-hearted and studious enthusiasm as you would in a match. In other words, there must be no aimless "anything-will-do-so-sling-'em-down" attitude about your practice.

At the nets always bowl the type of ball you prefer as your own style, for here you have the opportunity to develop your action, your change of pace, your run-up and your length.

Remember, too, that there is inspiration in emulation, I mentioned that factor when dealing with batting, if you remember, and it is equally true of bowling and bowlers. You can learn much from watching the first-class County bowlers in action, particularly those who use your own bowling style. Study their action, take note of everything they do, and then, next time you go to the nets, try to imitate their methods. It is no disgrace to follow a star.

Up to this point we have talked of bowling in a general way, but now let us delve into the subject in more detail.

What is the first thing that any bowler—I repeat ANY bowler—must develop? There is only one answer, for every bowler I have ever met has been convinced that the No. 1 fundamental in all bowling is length, in fact I will go so far as to say that it is the foundation of all bowling, the essential to all wicket-taking. No batsman, however experienced, can afford to take liberties with balls of perfect length.

Now what is perfect length? Actually it means merely pitching the ball up in such a way that the batsman can only play it with perfect safety by making a forward defensive shot.

Length doesn't just happen. You must work for it. Length must be developed and practice is the only way to perfection. I mastered it by placing a piece of paper on the spot that I considered was a good length—about 18 inches short of a half volley is about the right spot. Having decided on the spot, I kept pegging away until I could drop almost every delivery right on to it.

Try it. It will mean a lot of hard work but it must be done, for without length you will make no progress as a bowler.

Length differs according to the state of the wicket. For instance the ball must be pitched up farther on a slow wicket. Why, you ask? Simply because the ball on a slow wicket is likely to stop suddenly after it pitches and will give the batsmen a chance to clout it. Thus it must be pitched up to make the batsman play forward, and oft-times he will lift it in consequence. A half volley is a good ball on a sticky wicket.

I have been caught off a half volley on a sticky wicket when trying to force a boundary off a ball that has stopped in this way.

After length comes action, another essential to good bowling.

Every coach will tell you that your action must be natural, easy and rhythmic, but there are a few fundamentals that must be followed.

First of all, for any type of bowling the left shoulder must be facing the batsman when the ball is delivered. (I speak of right-handed bowlers, of course.) Keep upright when you deliver, with your left leg stiff; hold your head erect, and reach for it with your bowling arm. Get this as high as you can.

Brush your ear with every delivery, and release the ball from the hand when the arm is at the top of its circling action, except for the very slow ball, which is delivered just before the hand reaches its highest point. But that is something that I will discuss later on, for only the bowler of experience can deliver that type of ball with any success.

The run-up to the wicket is really part of the bowling action and it must also be given close study, but without seeing you bowl it would be well-nigh impossible for me to give you any personal advice about your own run-up. It is a matter for the individual to decide his most effective run-up. I should like to impress you, however, with the need to adopt a run that is natural, easy and executed with a smooth rhythmic action.

Any fault in your run-up, any stumbling, any hesitation at the moment of delivery will completely spoil your whole bowling action.

I have coached boys who have hesitated midway through their run-up to the wicket and then they have wondered why they have been "no-balled" or why they have delivered a bad ball. Stumbling, hesitation or complicated hops and jumps can be fatal, particularly to fast bowlers, for they lose half their speed if their run-up is stilted or broken in its rhythm.

Decide on a natural, straight run-up to the wicket, with a nice easy action to follow and you should succeed. Your run-up and delivery should become second nature to you. You should never need to pause or hesitate when you have once started your run. It should all be automatic, and it will become so if you put in sufficient practice.

Some fastish bowlers take too long a run and tire themselves out sooner than they need. To those fellows I would say, cut down your run and learn to do more with the ball.

Many of you will remember Morris Nichols, my

comrade in so many Essex matches. I recollect when "Nick," as a young man, had a clumsy run that started way back near the sight-screen. He was advised to cut down that run and make the ball do more of the work. He did so and he became a far better bowler following the change in his style, in fact he became one of the most valuable fast bowlers in the game.

Alf Gover, a Surrey stalwart for so many years, is another of the well-known pace bowlers who benefited considerably from a shortened run and more body action.

Fast bowlers should not sacrifice length for speed. So don't try to force your deliveries by bowling faster than your natural action will allow. It isn't the bowler with the longest run who bowls the fastest ball, you know. A long dash up to the wicket—shock tactics we call it in big cricket—may look terrifying to the batsman, but the fellow who races up to the bowling crease like a runaway whirlwind is more likely to be erratic and expensive in the matter of "extras" than the man who always bowls well within himself, preferring length with controlled pace to mere speed.

Maurice Tate, the Sussex and England Test bowler, took only about four paces, but he appeared faster, because of his pace off the pitch, than most of the so-called pace bowlers, men taking a much longer run-up. You see, Maurice had developed such a perfect natural action that he got the full swing of his body behind his deliveries, and because he conserved his energies so well he was able to do almost anything he wanted with the ball when he strode up to the crease.

Tate was fast off the wicket, no doubt about that. When he hit a batsman on the leg, as he did more than once, that man usually felt the blow for days afterwards, but it was only his wonderful body action that gave him such fierce pace off the pitch. It was certainly not because he took a long run. He had such wonderful command of length that he sometimes bowled a slower ball with exactly the same action, which had the batsman playing forward too soon, often with fatal results.

Maurice Tate, incidentally, was the finest seam bowler I ever faced. He had everything and he could have bowled all day long, as he often did. He was as dangerous and as accurate at the end of an innings as at the beginning. But then the Sussex bowler had been well trained in the arts of bowling and his success came from concentrated practice.

That is the hallmark of the good bowler—hard work and no slacking.

VII

Cricket's "Spin-sters"

MY COACHING experience has proved that, contrary to general opinion, more young bowlers are keen on spin than on fast bowling. That gives me a great deal of pleasure, for I specialised in spin and took hundreds of wickets with that type of bowling.

My father was a spin bowler and from my earliest boyhood I set out to emulate him, which made me something of a natural spinner.

The speed merchants of cricket often appear the more spectacular, but records prove that it is the slower bowlers who usually earn more dividends in the way of wickets. Please do not run away with the idea that I am not an admirer of the good pace bowler; I am merely stating facts that can be proved.

You see, invariably the fast bowler is at his best only when the shine is still on the ball, but once he has accomplished his work at the start of an innings, it is time for the spinners to take over the attack, though the fast bowlers will be brought on again to finish off the innings.

I will not spend time trying to tell you how to bowl the leg and off breaks. Study the accompanying photographs and you will see how the ball is held for these two types of delivery. The success of either depends entirely upon the right grip, allied to perfect length.

The leg break, my favourite, is equivalent to an out-swinger. For that reason it is a most dangerous ball, from the batsman's point of view, for it leaves the bat

—runs away—and is always likely to be edged into the slips.

There are one or two salient points which the spin bowler should note. I always advise young spinners to use the crease as much as possible; in other words, don't bowl every ball from the same spot. Thus the ball will be delivered at the batsman from different angles. But length is vital to the success of spin bowling and I like to see the ball pitched about middle and off, so that the batsman must play it.

I cannot repeat that axiom too often—*you must make the batsman play the ball all the time*. To do that you must pitch it well up to him by giving the ball plenty of air.

That brings me to a phase of spin—or slow—bowling that is the subject of many questions to me when I am coaching at the nets. The subject is flighting the ball.

What is flight? It merely means bowling with a very high action and allowing the ball to leave the hand just behind your head. This causes the ball to hang in the air and has the effect of making the batsman think the ball is to pitch closer to him than it eventually does. It gets him in two minds and often the hasty shot he plays is a fatal shot.

Flight bowling, actually, is a definite type of attack and some bowlers prefer it to concentrated spin, although flight must be allied to spin or swing for it to be really effective and successful.

On plumb easy wickets, when the pitch does not give assistance to spin, the flight bowler may still be dangerous, for he will be able to make the ball do the work in the air instead of on the ground.

The flighted ball should always be bowled into the wind.

This has the effect of making it hang longer and keeps the batsman in constant suspense. Incidentally, it is difficult to flight a ball in warmer climates as the air is too thin and too dry. That is why the Australian and South African slow bowlers rely mainly on spin, and right well they do it, too.

The main reason for this preference for spin, however, is that the wickets in Australia and South Africa particularly are so perfect that bowlers out there must work and practice really hard as it takes a great deal of spin on such wickets to make the ball turn a little. Because of this they become real masters of their art, as is proved by the undeniable fact that Australia and South Africa have produced many spin bowlers who are among the world's greatest.

Whether you prefer flight alone or flight with spin, however, the slower type of bowler must be always endeavouring to make the ball do something, either in the air or on the ground. Do that and you won't go far wrong.

Slow bowling must never become stereotyped. If you have mastered the arts of your job you should be able to mix your deliveries and keep the batsmen guessing. Vary your pace and don't spin every ball. Learn to send down a straight one whilst still using the same finger grip, to hoodwink the batsman.

A genuine leg break sometimes becomes a top spinner because of the state of the pitch, but there have been— and are—spin bowlers who deliberately use the top spinner as one of their stock deliveries. Used sparingly, this delivery will always keep the batsman in two minds.

"Tich" Freeman, that wonderful little man who took thousands of wickets for Kent, bowled it as well as anyone

I ever met. But then Freeman was able to mix them so adroitly, using the leg break, the googly and the top spinner with such uncanny accuracy and such perfect length, that he was a law unto himself.

He would give a batsman a leg break or two and then, just when you thought you knew what was coming at you, he would completely hoodwink you by sending down a top spinner with his usual leg break action. It was most difficult to pick out that ball.

Talking of top spinners reminds me of one amazing incident in my life. Playing for Essex against Middlesex at Leyton I was bowling my usual leg breaks, but because of some peculiarity of the wicket, every now and again a delivery would go straight through without turning an inch. That ball certainly proved a terror to the batsmen and I sent seven men back to the pavilion l.b.w. Each of them played for the break which they knew I was trying to impart to the ball, and each of them put his leg in front of a top spinner.

After the sixth man had been dismissed in that manner, Harry Butt, who was umpiring, said to me:

"Look here, Jack, you'll make yourself dry saying 'How's that?' When you get inside again you'd better have my cup of tea as well as your own. I've put my arm up so often that I shan't be able to raise it any more."

The googly is another very difficult ball for the batsman to face—and for the bowler to bowl.

It is really an off break bowled with an almost similar action to the leg break, for the ball leaves the back of the hand instead of the front. For this reason quite a number of batsmen who fail to watch the bowler's hand play for a leg break only to find the ball turn into them instead of away from them.

The googly on its own is a wasted ball. Combined with the leg break, however, it can be most devastating. However, if you bowl the googly, do not use it more than twice in an over. Overdo this type of ball and the batsman will be watching and waiting for it, but use it sparingly and you will keep him on tenterhooks all the time.

The googly is a natural gift. Bowlers of this ball are born and not made. Proof of this is in the fact that effective googly bowlers are few and far between.

R. W. V. Robins, the former Middlesex skipper, used it with great success and now, strangely enough, Middlesex have introduced us to a young man who bids fair to become one of the finest exponents of the googly this country has ever produced. I refer to young Ian Bedford, who played his first County match last season at the age of 17. I have seen Ian bowling his googly and he shows every promise of even greater things to come.

Just a word now about left arm spinners. These fellows are worth their weight in wickets to any side, for the left arm spinner bowls with an off break action which becomes a leg break to a right-handed batsman, and that can be a most awkward ball to play effectively. For proof of this you have only to appreciate the consistent success of such men as Dick Howorth, of Worcester; Jack Young, of Middlesex; and Sam Cook, of Gloucestershire, to name only three of the modern left arm "spin-sters."

If it were possible, I should like to see at least one left arm spin bowler included in every team.

There is still one ball of the spin variety that we have not yet mentioned—it is "The Chinaman." It is bowled by left handers using a leg break action, which produces an off break to a right handed batsman. It is not a very

F

popular delivery among bowlers. Its success depends entirely upon perfect length.

Fleetwood Smith, the Australian, used to bowl it with good effect, and nowadays its chief exponent is Denis Compton.

I am not going to suggest that young bowlers try to develop this type of ball, but under the new l.b.w. rule, bowled by a man who has complete control of his spin deliveries, it can pay dividends.

As one of the chaps of whom it could not be said "They toil not neither do they spin," I have always been most interested in other bowlers of my type. Having met all the masters of spin of recent years, memories of them crowd upon me.

The greatest left arm spinner I ever played against was Charlie Parker, of Gloucestershire. Some of you living in the North may wonder why I do not plump for the late Hedley Verity, the masterly Yorkshire bowler who followed in the footsteps of Wilfred Rhodes, the greatest of them all. Verity undoubtedly was a great spinner, but Parker was more difficult to play.

On a sticky wicket, Charlie Parker was veritably unplayable, and he was capable of running through the strongest of batting sides. If he had had the co-operation of such a brilliant fielding side as Verity had with Yorkshire, he would have been the greatest left-arm spin bowler the cricket world had ever known. As I shall try to prove to you in a future chapter, a first-class fielding side can make the moderate bowler into a side wrecker.

Tom Goddard was the best off-spinner of my time, and despite his age he is still a bowler to be feared, for his performances last season were exceptional. Being so tall, he is able to flight the ball from such a height that he makes it lift, and an off break that gets up off a good length is a most difficult ball for a batsman to play with any confidence.

The most awkward spinner, from the batsman's point of view, was Bill O'Reilly, the tall Australian. Unlike most spinners bred in the British climate, he did not flight the ball. He also bowled a good deal faster than the majority of spinners, and his record of wickets in Test cricket is proof enough of his amazing ability. Like all the great Australian bowlers, his length was immaculate and his control of spin and change of pace were matched only by his colleague in so many Tests, Clarrie Grimmett.

The last named, by the way, spent several years spinning a ball and mastering his length in his back garden before he made his mark in the top flight of international cricket. Owing to the perfect pitches on which he had to bowl, this constant practice was necessary, but you can all learn a lesson from Grimmett's perseverance and his painstaking determination to become master of his art.

Much of the advice given to spin bowlers is also applicable to those who prefer to bowl fast. The finger grip is different, as you will see from the photograph following page 68, but perfect command of length is just as vital. I cannot emphasise too much that this is the basis of success in ALL types of bowling.

It is essential for the fast bowler to keep the ball well up to the batsman while the ball is new, for if it is pitched well up, it is longer in the air and the longer the ball is in the air the more time it will have to swing.

What is a swinging ball? Quite simple really. It is a ball that swings or dips as it travels through the air. The really deadly ball is the one that travels straight through the air for most of its trajectory and then dips or swings over the last yard or two. If it is swinging all the way, the batsman has more time to follow its flight.

This swinging motion is caused by the action of the air on the moving ball. The side with the pronounced shine presents less resistance to the air and so moves slightly faster than the rougher side. If, for instance, you hold the ball with the shine to the right, the ball will swing to the left, because its right side is moving rather faster through the air. If there were no difference between the surface of the two sides of the ball, it would not swing in this way.

That is why it is so necessary for the pace bowler to keep the shine on the ball for as long as possible. You must have seen the fast bowlers polishing one side of the ball on their flannels as they walk back to their mark.

The fielders can do much to assist the bowler to retain the shine on the ball by keeping it off the ground as much as possible and throwing it direct to the wicket keeper, who will pass it back to the bowler by way of the hands of the close-in fielders.

There are two forms of swing delivery—the out-swinger, and the in-swinger. Let us study them one at a time.

The out-swinger, sometimes known as the away-swinger, is a ball that swings from the leg to the off. It is bowled with the right foot close up to the bowling wicket. (See diagram.) The ball is held with the orthodox seam grip, with the shine on the right. As the ball leaves the hand the body must follow through, with the arm swinging across the body from right to left, which is the direction the ball takes as it travels through the air. The body and arm follow-through are essential.

The in-swinger, the ball that swings from the off to

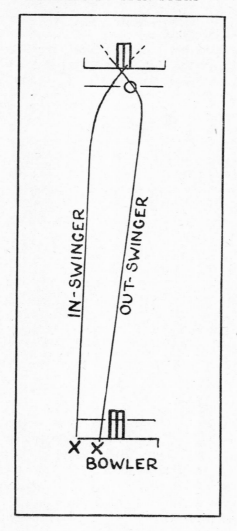

leg, is bowled with the same finger grip, except that the shine this time must be on the left of the ball. Unlike the out-swinger, it is bowled wide of the crease and the swing is obtained from the arm being high and the body slightly bent to the left, because with this type of delivery the body cannot follow through with the ball as with the out-swinger.

The swing bowler must make full use of the wind. It should be apparent, if you give it a moment's thought, that it will help the ball to move from right to left—and *vice versa*, of course—if the wind is blowing across the pitch in much the same direction. That is why the swing bowler should always be asked by his captain to choose the end from which he would prefer to bowl.

Accurate swing bowling is definitely effective, and we are not likely to recover our former prestige in Test cricket until we can find a pace bowler or two of that type to open the attack. Swing bowling on the right occasion can be just as deadly as spin on a sticky wicket. I found the out-swinger that dipped late was often a wicket-shatterer, in fact I would say that it is the most difficult ball of all to play.

Just a word on a few of the noted pace bowlers I faced during my active years in cricket, The fastest of them all was Harold Larwood. He was deadly during the opening overs of a match and his accuracy was phenomenal. A batsman needed the eyes of a hawk and the nimble footwork of a featherweight boxer to make any impression against Larwood, for his length was immaculate.

I am never likely to forget the Notts express, for it was an injury received from one of Larwood's fastest deliveries that lost me my chance of a trip to Australia. It was in a Test trial between teams representing the South and the

North at Manchester in 1932. With my score at 9, I mistimed a Larwood special. The ball cracked me on the hand as I tried to hook it. It gave me plenty of pain but I batted on and had reached 51 not out when D. R. Jardine, the South skipper, declared the innings closed.

When I returned to the pavilion my hand had swollen to such proportions that Sir Pelham Warner advised me to have it X-rayed. This was done and to my dismay the examination revealed that I had broken my finger. I place no blame upon Larwood, but that injury laid me aside for many weeks and I could not be considered for the following winter's tour "Down Under."

Mention of Larwood recalls a memorable century I scored in 1936 against Notts at Clacton. Larwood was in devastating form, and when you know that Bill Voce, the other member of the Nottingham "speed twins," was at the opposite end, you will not be surprised when I say that I was jumping about like a cat on hot bricks for most of the innings and picking balls "off my eyebrows." However, I collected 111 runs, a century that gave me a great deal of satisfaction.

Larwood was a great cricketer, but the best fast bowler I ever played against, the master of them all in my opinion, was MacDonald, the big Australian, who afterwards bowled so well for Lancashire. "Mac" was an artist and he made the ball do so much at speed that he always had the batsman thinking hard.

The Australian touring side of 1921 was one of the finest teams ever to visit these shores, for in addition to MacDonald they had Jack Gregory, a wonderful all-rounder. Actually I should say that Gregory was the most terrifying fast bowler of this century. He was a giant in stature and he took a terrific run and bowled from such a height that he could make even good length balls fly up around a batsman's face.

More than one young batsman got himself out through sheer terror when opposed to Jack Gregory. Sure he was fast, a human typhoon, but a really great bowler for all that.

Having mentioned my former Essex colleague, Morris Nichols, several times already in this book, I will not say much more about this remarkable cricketer, except to state that he made the ball do more than any specialist pace bowler I ever met. If "Nick" had had Larwood's speed—for he certainly had the accuracy and the un-flagging enthusiasm—he would have been a world beater, for he always bowled at the stumps and could never be accused of using shock tactics.

I cannot let this opportunity pass without mentioning one of the finest demonstrations of pace bowling I ever witnessed. It was in a match against Yorkshire, at Huddersfield in 1935. Essex dismissed the mighty Yorkshire side for 31, to provide the season's sensation. The men who accomplished this remarkable performance were Nichols and H. D. Read, who would have reached the heights of fame in Test cricket if he could have given more time to the game.

In that memorable match, Read was in such devastating form that he took 6 wickets for 11 runs, while "Nick" took the other four for 17 and then followed this with 7 in the second innings for 37 runs. That was fast bowling at its best and it shocked Yorkshire. (By the way, Essex won that amazing match by an innings and 204 runs.)

Bowlers can be placed into separate classes according to their type of delivery, but the men in each of these specialist classes are not produced from the same mould.

Fast bowler's grip.

Leg break grip.

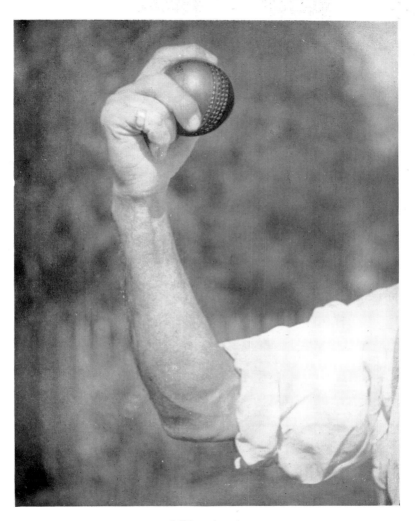

Off break grip.

Grip for the googly.

There are some bowlers who make the ball do unaccountable things through some peculiarity in their action.

I mention this because I had the coaching of a young player who took a number of wickets with a very peculiar ball, yet he did not know how or why he bowled that particular ball, and I certainly could not discover the reason. However, I did not try, and I advised him not to be too inquisitive about his own speciality, either, for I held a very vivid memory of a famous Essex bowler of a past decade.

This fine cricketer bowled a ball that took wickets, to the amazement and wonder of comrades and opponents alike. This particular ball puzzled him so much that he spent hours on his own trying to fathom the reason for it. That curiosity was his undoing. Through his own insatiable desire to learn more about his own peculiar delivery he completely lost all his natural bowling ability and in a short time he was finished as a County cricketer.

If this ever happens to you, as it might, leave well alone. If you cannot discover the reason for some uncanny peculiarity in your bowling, it is almost certain that the batsmen will not be able to find a counter for it. So keep it up your sleeve as a trump card.

There is little more to be said about bowling, except for me to offer one or two more general tips by way of conclusion.

When you are not bowling, study the batsmen. By doing so you should be able to learn quite a lot about an opponent's pet strokes and his like or dislike of certain types of delivery, and when next you take the ball you will be armed with knowledge that you should be able to turn to good use.

If you see that a batsman is inclined to any particular stroke, then it is up to you, the bowler, to feed him with deliveries which he can play in his own pet way. Before you do that, however, bring up another fielder to cover that stroke. Even if you fail to tempt the batsman into playing into your hands—or rather the fielder's—at least you should be able to force him to change his natural stroke and play shots that he does not make naturally or confidently.

In this connection I recall a match against Lancashire, in which I was scoring a great many runs with drives wide of mid-on, a favourite stroke of mine. George Duckworth, the inimitable little Lancashire stumper, saw this and caused another man to be brought up on the on-side. Thus, with virtually two mid-ons, my run-getting on that side of the wicket was strictly limited and I was forced to seek other avenues in my efforts to score. That move cut down my rate of scoring considerably.

There is far more in bowling than just slinging the ball down at the batsmen, you know. Cricket is a battle of wits between the batsman and the bowler. Brute force doesn't count in cricket and the bowler without brains is never likely to take many wickets.

Guile counts, and the successful bowler must have the mental capacity to weigh up every situation quickly as it presents itself and to devise some means to tackle it promptly.

Many a batsman—myself included—has been dismissed by being caught out, bowled or stumped, but in some of these instances the scorebook should have read "Thought out by the bowler," because the fellow with the ball was sufficiently equipped mentally to be able to force the batsmen into making a shot that lost him his wicket.

LEG-BREAK

On a sticky wicket (A) the bowler would use a silly mid-off and move third man to gulley. On a hard wicket (B) gulley would be moved to third man and silly mid-off would be placed at deep square leg.

THIRD MAN (B)

SLIP

W. K.

GULLEY (A)

DEEP SQ. LEG (B)

SHORT SQ. LEG

COVER

SILLY MID-OFF (A)

BOWLER

EXTRA COVER

MID-OFF

MID-ON

LONG OFF

The ball is propelled by body and limb co-ordination but the mainspring is the brain behind the actual motive power.

There are many ways of bowling with your brains. It may be that at one end is a batsman against whom you can make little impression, but his partner at the wickets is a man you feel you could tempt into a stroke that will send him back to the pavilion, a man, maybe, who has shown a dislike to your own style of bowling. All right, there is only one thing to be done. You must entice the better of the two batsmen to score a single, by giving him the right ball and moving a fielder so that he can take only one run off the stroke that you make him play. That will force the man who dislikes your bowling to the batting end—and the rest will be up to you.

Don't be one-track-minded in your bowling. Vary your deliveries according to the state of the wicket on which you are playing and—here is one of the most important of all essentials to bowling success—bring your fielders into your bowling strategy.

First of all, do you know how to place your field in the most effective manner? It is useless to have men standing about in the field doing nothing. Remember, a good fielding side can make a moderate bowler into a side-wrecker. But that can happen only if the field is correctly placed to cover the majority of strokes which will be made from your particular type of bowling.

There are orthodox fields for each bowling style, and I have set them out for you in diagram form. The placing of any of those set fields should fairly efficiently cover most strokes which the batsmen are likely to make, but I must point out that the bowler of experience does not always

OFF-BREAK

This field is set for a fast wicket. On a sticky wicket third man would be moved to slip on the leg side.

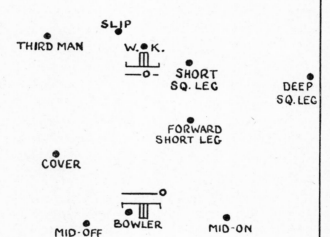

adhere strictly to the orthodox in the placing of his fielders.

The good bowler will not hesitate to change his field to counter the particular style of the batsman to whom he is bowling. If the fellow with the bat shows a partiality for one particular stroke, then it is up to the bowler to cover it by the moving of a fielder, as I have illustrated to you already.

Every bowler should know from experience what field he wants and he should endeavour to make the batsmen play to that field.

In this connection, remember that it is easier for the batsman to play the ball in the direction in which it is swinging or turning than to any other part of the field. For instance, off-break bowling brings most runs on the on side. Because of this, always place most of your fielders on the side of the pitch which will see most of the ball after it leaves the bat. That should be quite obvious, yet I have seen plenty of young bowlers who have not learned this elementary lesson.

Don't waste fielders. Quite a number of leg break bowlers religiously place a man at square leg. I admit I have put a fielder there in my diagram of the field lay-out for the leg break bowler, but actually you know, if the bowler is sure of his length and direction, there is no need for a man at square leg, for no batsman can hit a good length leg break pitched on the wicket with any certainty to square leg.

In that case, a man in that particular position would be more or less wasted. At the same time, I have known plenty of leg spinners, men who were not quite masters of their art to be absolutely sure of their length and direction, who could not bowl with any degree of

FAST

DEEP FINE LEG

THIRD
MAN (DEEP)

1st. SLIP

2nd. SLIP

GULLEY

W.K.

SHORT
SQ. LEG

COVER

SHORT
MID-ON

BOWLER

MID-OFF

confidence, unless they had a square leg. Under those circumstances the placing of a man in that position would be justified.

You must remember that I am trying to tell you the CORRECT way to do things, but I know quite well that the orthodox is not always the method chosen by everyone. But if you have full command of length, and direction and the confidence to bowl leg spinners, then bowl without a fielder at square leg.

The use of too many deep fielders to slow or spin bowling is further evidence that the bowler lacks confidence and that he is content to allow the batsmen to attack HIM instead of himself attacking the batsmen.

When I was just a youthful member of the Essex team I was put on to bowl my leg spinners and Johnnie Douglas, the skipper, asked me what field I wanted. I detailed the various positions I wanted covered and came to the leg side.

"I'll have a deep square leg," I said. But the skipper pulled me up very abruptly.

"Oh, no, you won't," came his sharp retort. "You'll bowl a length and leave the leg side open. They'll only hit you out there off long hops or full tosses, but not off good length stuff."

That set me thinking, but in years to come those words of Johnnie Douglas were proved.

Good bowlers will often leave a gap deliberately in the field when they know that a batsman shows a partiality for one particular shot. The batsman is then fed with deliveries which he cannot naturally hit in that direction, but ten chances to one he will keep trying to sneak one through the gap in the field by hitting against the break. Invariably that will bring about his downfall.

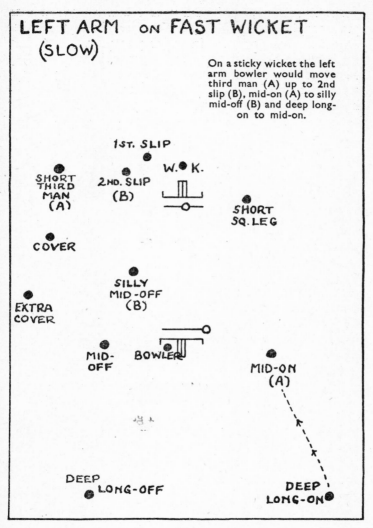

LEFT ARM ON FAST WICKET (SLOW)

On a sticky wicket the left arm bowler would move third man (A) up to 2nd slip (B), mid-on (A) to silly mid-off (B) and deep long-on to mid-on.

1ST. SLIP

W. K.

SHORT THIRD MAN (A)

2ND. SLIP (B)

SHORT SQ. LEG

COVER

SILLY MID-OFF (B)

EXTRA COVER

BOWLER

MID-OFF

MID-ON (A)

DEEP LONG-OFF

DEEP LONG-ON

So, to sum up, bowl with your brains as well as with your body. Watch points and take note of everything that goes on in every match in which you play. Remember, the bowler should call the tune and make the batsmen play it. When the position is reversed it is time for the bowler to take stock of himself and find out what is wrong with his deliveries. That is bowling with your brains.

VIII

Fielding can be Fun

MANY MATCHES have been won by good fielding. Yes, and just as many games have been lost through bad work in the field. It matters little what the grade of match, good fielding will always bring its own reward.

As a matter of fact, there should be no really bad fielding. There will always be outstanding batsmen and poor batsmen, good bowlers and others who could not take a wicket if they tried for years, but EVERY cricketer should be a sound fielder.

Go more deeply into this question. There are usually reasons for a man failing with the bat or the ball, but there can never be a sound reason for slipshod or slovenly fielding.

Despite the individualistic nature of batting and bowling, cricket is first and foremost a team game, and in no phase does the value of team work count for more than in the field. Look at it this way. A poor fielder who gives away a number of runs is owing his team runs when he goes in to bat. Thus, even if he hits up fifty but has previously given twenty-five away, his score is worth only half its actual figure. That is not match-winning cricket.

There should be no place in any team for an indifferent fielder, whatever his other attributes. I have known men who have been played for their fielding alone. I could also tell you of really good batsmen, and bowlers, too, who have been dropped by their skippers because they could not hold their own in the field, in County cricket, too.

So don't neglect fielding. It is of the utmost importance if your team is to follow the winning way.

Wherever you are fielding you should always be on your toes, poised ready to make a swift dive either way, or to race after the ball as it speeds past you on its way towards the boundary. In that connection never take anything for granted. Chase every ball to the boundary, no matter how fast it is travelling and how futile the chase may seem. Remember that four runs cannot be signalled until the ball has CROSSED the line.

Always watch the ball, the bowler and the batsman. Try to anticipate what the ball is likely to do when it leaves the bat. By doing so you will be halfway to saving the shot long before the ball reaches you. All fielders, except the slips and the other close-in men, should begin to walk slowly towards the wicket as the bowler begins his run-up, ready to nip in and gather the ball without waste of a second. This often prevents the batsmen attempting a snappy single.

There is one rule which all fielders should observe. It is this: never use one hand if you can get both hands to the ball. Safety first should be the motto. This is essential in the case of picking up. Use both hands whenever possible, and if the ball is coming straight towards you at speed, keep your heels together. The reason is obvious —yes, to prevent the ball slipping through the hands AND through your open legs, which is almost certain to add runs to your opponents' score. And every run counts.

There are occasions, of course, when you must execute a swift one-handed pick-up; for instance, when you stretch out for a ball streaking past you, or when you are running beside a ball that is streaking to the boundary.

Confidence and perfect timing are vital when you attempt a one-handed snatch.

Pick up and throw in all in the same action, for this, too, may save valuable runs, or even get a man run out. So many young players pick up the ball quite smartly, only to pause and then wind themselves up before slinging in to the wicket, thus wasting valuable seconds.

Throwing in correctly and accurately is most important. The right way is to throw the ball direct into the wicket keeper's hands about waist high, or just above stump height, so that he can gather it and whip off the bails (if that action is necessary), in one action and without a moment's delay. If, however, you are fielding so deep that you cannot throw to the wicket keeper full pitch, get it to him in one bounce, or, better still, throw it to a colleague who is backing up, so that he can sling it direct to the stumper.

Backing up is another important point to watch. Fielders should always be prepared to back up when the ball is thrown in. Cover up, too. If one fielder misses the ball, another in close proximity should be moving to cover his comrade. That is team spirit again.

Now we come to catching, a vital part of fielding work, for dropped catches can make such a great difference to the result of any game. Even Test matches have been won and lost because of missed catches at a crucial stage of the game.

I recall a match some years ago. Essex wickets were falling fast in the last innings, and I was doggedly trying to stave off the rot that was setting in. Fielders crowded round the bat and then, to my dismay, a ball popped up and I spooned it into the hands of a fielder. Next instant my dismay turned to delight—he put it on the floor.

I made the most of that let-off and, in addition to collecting a half hundred, we managed to hit off the runs needed for victory. If that catch had been held, we should most likely have lost the match.

In catching it is as well to remember the oft-quoted rule—two hands are better than one. Of course, as in everything, there are certain exceptions, occasions when fielders must make a swift dive to the ball in an effort to bring off a catch one-handed. If such a chance presents itself, however slender it may appear, you must make the effort without hesitation. If the ball sticks, then you'll be the hero of the side. If you miss, at least you will not be blamed for attempting the 100 to 1 chance.

Learn to catch the ball correctly. The hands should be cupped with both palms facing upwards and with the fingers slightly bent, but not rigid. Keep the hands as close to the body as possible and allow the ball to come to you. There must be no snatch and grab, above all behind the wicket.

Always get well underneath a high, dropping ball and keep your eyes fixed on it as it falls. As the ball reaches you, let the hands give slightly with the momentum of the ball, and hug it to your chest to prevent it hopping out.

Go for every catch with confidence, no matter how hopeless you feel it is. Most of us can recall some marvellous catches, half chances that would have brought no blame to the fielder if they had been missed.

I remember seeing the late Cambridge and Essex all-rounder, Claude Ashton, a brilliant field anywhere "in the country," run yards in an effort to hold a flying ball that was sailing straight for the boundary ropes. It was any odds against him even reaching the ball, but to our amazement, he got his hands around it right at his feet, turned a somersault and then sprang upright again with the ball still glued to his palms. Nine out of ten fielders would have let that ball go—but not Claude Ashton.

Another of these miracle catches, was one that sent me back to the pavilion. We were playing Surrey at the Oval and with my eye well in I was attacking the bowling. Down came a short ball. I pivoted and hooked it as hard as I could, hoping to see it go crashing to the boundary. But Bill Hitch was fielding at short leg, and Bill was the finest fielder in that position I ever saw. Anyway, Bill leapt into the air, flung up one hand, just as though he were picking an apple off a tree, and with all the nonchalance in the world he hung on to that stinging hook of mine.

That was just about the finest catch I ever saw, and Bill Hitch never lets me forget it. Every time we meet he mentions it.

This is not to be wondered at for nothing gives a cricketer greater satisfaction than the holding of a particularly difficult catch. It's grand to put up a good score with the bat or to see the stumps spread-eagled from a ball you have bowled, but to take a catch that everyone expects you to miss—yes, that's a really memorable moment to any cricketer.

Many a catch is worth as much to a side as a big score from the bat, but, unfortunately from the bowler's point of view, every chance is not held.

Every cricketer has brought off brilliant catches, and every cricketer, no matter whether he plays for a junior side or for his country, could tell you of the sitters he placed on the carpet! Every cricketer drops catches. I have missed plenty, and so will you before you complete your cricket career, but don't let a mistake of this kind upset your game, no matter how vital it is. No one is more sorry about a dropped catch than the fellow who drops it. So if it happens to you, then grin and bear it and make up your mind that you will make a better effort when you are offered another chance.

Talking of catches reminds me of another incident that happened to me in my younger days. A ball was hit high into the air and I began to race towards the spot where I thought it would drop, my eyes turned skywards. Suddenly something hit me a mighty whack and I found myself flat on my back. I had collided with another fielder who had the same intention as myself—to catch that ball. We caught one another instead, and the ball nearly buried itself in the ground!

When two fielders go for the same ball it is best for the captain to shout to one of them by name to leave the catch to the other.

Here is another point worth noting. Any high ball near the wicket should be left to the keeper. Remember, he is wearing gloves and that makes a heap of difference.

Now a few words might not be out of place regarding the attributes necessary for the successful filling of the most important positions in the field. In this connection every player should decide on his most effective place in the field, and to stick to it whenever possible. Fielders should be adaptable, but in fielding as in most things, it is every fellow to his own job.

For some years after I had become established in the Essex County side, I was regarded as the team's cover point and made the position my own until one day, in emergency, I was switched from cover to the slips. Before many overs had been bowled I had dropped a catch, and only because I was strange to my new position.

If you stick to one position in the field you accustom yourself to the way the ball comes through to you and you form definite views on the handling of all shots that come to that position. Change your berth and you are forced to alter all your experienced fielding opinions.

Cover point is, in my opinion, the most onerous position in the field, because of the great amount of work that is thrown upon the man in that position. It calls for a player who is quick on his feet, and agile, with a lightning pick-up and an accurate throw. Cover point is a busy man, for he is seldom inactive during an innings. The speed of his action can prevent many of those quick singles which give so much pleasure to batsmen.

The best cover point I ever saw was Jack Hobbs. Very little passed his eager hands; his anticipation, and his brilliant throws, straight into the hands of little Herbert Strudwick, the Surrey stumper, had to be seen to be believed. Jack saved nearly as many runs as he scored.

Among modern players I should say that Cyril Washbrook, of Lancashire, has no equal at cover. In the Test matches in Australia two years ago, he saved hundreds of runs with his wonderful anticipation, split-second timing in picking up and his speed of action.

Next on the list for importance I should say are the slips, the "right hand men" of the pace bowlers. The successful slip fielder must be always on the alert; his eye must never leave the ball for a second, but, what is even more important, he must have a safe and sure pair of hands, for more catches find their way into the waiting hands of the slips than to any other of the fielders.

You may have noticed that many of cricket's greatest batsmen were—and are—among the finest slip fielders.

This, perhaps, is not surprising. The great batsman is outstanding because he has such a keen eye and is naturally quick to snap into instantaneous action. The same faculties are of paramount importance in the slips.

Wally Hammond, brilliant batsman, was the prince of slip-catchers, in my opinion. He was so swift and so sure that the ball often seemed to be held in his safe hands before it had left the bat. At least, that was the impression it gave to the spectators, and even to the batsman. Hammond's "bag" of catches was certainly phenomenal.

Reg Taylor, one of my Essex comrades for some years, was another of these open-handed fellows who missed little in the slips.

It was Chipperfield, the Australian, who made the greatest slip catch I ever saw. It sent me back to the pavilion.

It was at Chelmsford in 1934, I cut a ball from Bill O'Reilly, that super-spinner with so many Test match honours, hard towards gulley; Chipperfield, who was the only slip, must have anticipated that stroke for he leapt yards sideways and took the ball one-handed as he sprawled full length on the turf. It was a brilliant catch and although it sent me back to the pavilion I felt like joining in the terrific round of applause that greeted it.

Slip fielders should always drop down into a stooping position before the ball leaves the bowler's hand, so that they are in a position to take a fast low ball, for it is easier to spring up to a high ball than to drop down suddenly to a ball that snicks off the bat at speed only inches above the turf.

Some bowlers, when not in action, prefer to field in the slips, but I maintain that a regular bowler should be placed at mid-on or mid-off. In the slips he would have a great deal of stooping and leg bending which would tire him unduly. The stock bowler should always conserve his energy, so a captain should not ask a regular bowler to field in the slips.

There are no other particular attributes for the fielding places, except that third man, deep fine leg and in fact any fielder "in the country," should be the fastest runners in the side and capable of throwing the ball direct to the stumper. Deep fielders should, of course, also be proficient at catching, but then you might as well say that is true of every man in every fielding side.

Joe Hardstaff, the Nottinghamshire Test star, was one of the greatest outfields of my acquaintance, but he has a brilliant rival for the honours these days in Denis Compton. The greatness of these players is hardly surprising, however, for both developed their speed and alertness on the football field.

Deep fielders should go as far back as possible, for it is easier to run forward to a ball than to scamper backwards, and if you are going deep, then you may as well go as deep as you can, for you will have far more chance of cutting off a ball before it reaches the boundary if you have any distance to run. It is also more advantageous to be in a position to run in than to run backwards for a catch in the long field.

Fielders must keep cool, calm and collected in everything they do. Flustered fieldsmen miss catches and in their fumbling haste give away runs that should never be scored. In no phase of fielding is it more imperative to keep a cool head than when trying to run out a batsman.

Speed is vital, for the difference between a batsman being "out" and "home" is often only a split second. But many a man has been allowed to scrape back to his crease because a fielder has thrown the ball to the wrong end. Watch that point carefully, for although the wicket keeper is usually in the better position to run a man out, there are occasions when it pays to sling the ball to the bowler's end—that is if the bowler or another fielder is in position to take the ball and whip off the bails.

It may be, however, that the bowler's wicket is "vacant" and the running batsman is still yards from the crease. Under those circumstances you must chance your arm and play a lone hand by letting fly at the stumps.

I remember an incident that happened at Leyton against Gloucestershire. Wally Hammond had scored 25 when I ran him out. It was like this, I fielded the ball about twenty yards from the bowler's wicket, which was not being covered by the bowler or a fielder. So although I was square with the stumps and, in consequence, could only see one of them, I tried my luck and let go.

To my delight the stumps were spreadeagled while Wally Hammond's bat was still some feet from the crease. I suppose it was lucky that I hit the stumps, but if I had not attempted it, Hammond would not have been out, and he might have gone on to record another of his many hundreds.

In taking direct action of that nature there is always a danger of overthrows, but the result often justifies the risk. In any case, it all depends upon the state of the game. For instance, if you were fielding and your opponents needed only a few runs to win, no fielder would dare to take the risk of aiming direct at the stumps, unless he was standing quite close to the wicket. If the ball missed and went for overthrows, that present of runs might make all the difference between victory and defeat.

Take your work in the field seriously and concentrate

just as much as you would if you were batting or bowling. And that reminds me, give the bowler as much assistance as you can, not only by holding the catches and retrieving every possible run, but by saving his back and legs from too much unnecessary strain.

What do I mean? Just this. When you return the ball to the bowler, fling it to him in the air and give him an easy catch. Never return the ball low or along the ground, for every time the bowler stoops he uses some of the valuable energy he needs for his bowling.

A little point, but it is the little points in cricket that often are forgotten.

All right then, let me see every young cricketer on his toes in the field, and, as with all other phases of the game, take every chance of practice. Yes, it's essential.

No County player would consider his pre-season preparation complete without indulging in several spells of fielding work. I certainly never missed a chance of such practice and since I have been coaching at Eton I have been very encouraged by the lads' fielding enthusiasm. We take part in a certain amount of fielding practice throughout the whole season.

All players, especially the slip fielders, should have a few hours' practice before the season starts—and on any other occasions when time allows throughout the season—on the slip catcher, or the cradle as we call it. If your club hasn't got one of these, then see if it is possible to acquire or borrow one. There is nothing better to give the lads some first-rate training for hand and eye, and some good fun, too.

There are other forms of fielding practice, of course, all of which should find a place in your pre-season preparation. For another, send your biggest hitter out into the middle of the field while the rest of the fellows place themselves around in the deep field. The batsman bangs the ball at all heights and to all parts of the field, and it is up to his comrades to "get their hands in." This is excellent catching practice.

There is no reason, either, why you should not indulge in a little sharp catching practice during a match to keep the fielders' eyes keen. When a wicket falls, borrow an old ball from one of the umpires and call some of the fellows to form a rough ring. One of you can start to sling the ball about from one to another—well, there is no need to tell you any more. I'm sure you've seen it done, or you may even have indulged in that form of practice. If you haven't, try it. It's good.

Get some throwing-in practice, too. Put up one stump, with the wicket keeper guarding it, and the other players, standing around at different distances, can "try their arm and their aim" by throwing the ball to the stumper at just the right height for him to whip it down as though taking off the bails. This is fine practice for the fielders and the wicket keeper, so it will serve a double purpose.

Never neglect an opportunity for some fielding practice, for I cannot emphasise too strongly that good fielding is just as important a factor towards victory as skilful bowling and first-class run-getting.

I have already mentioned Yorkshire's brilliant fielding. From 1922 onwards the Northern County were Champions on twelve occasions. During that wonderful period they had good batsmen, they had skilful bowlers, some of the finest in the game, but every member of those sides was a sound fielder. I will go so far as to say that the Yorkshire fieldwork was so good that it made their bowlers 50 per cent. better than they might have been had they been poorly supported in the field.

It is perhaps a little unfair to single out any one of those fine Yorkshire fielders for special mention, but of them all Arthur Mitchell was really outstanding. He was certainly one of the greatest fielders in cricket and he took dozens of catches while fielding close in to the wicket. No man has ever fielded closer to the bat.

Good fielding—in fact, often miraculous fielding—has always been a prominent feature of the cricket of the Australians, and I am afraid the men from "Down Under" have often revealed the English fielding in a poor light in Test matches.

First class work in the field is a match-winning factor. There is no doubt about that.

There is just as much enjoyment and real pleasure in fielding as in batting and bowling; at least there should be if you have the right outlook on the game and the right degree of enthusiasm.

IX

The Man Behind The Stumps

FROM GENERAL fielding I turn now to the work of the wicket keeper, for the efforts of the rest of the fielders and the bowlers can be completely spoiled by a poor stumper.

I have never kept wicket and I don't know that I have ever wanted the job, for I consider the position of wicket keeper is the hardest and most onerous place in the whole field, calling for very special attributes. I have watched the work of so many keepers and they have my admiration and respect.

The stumper cannot relax for a moment, except between overs. He must concentrate all the time and be alive, alert and always on his toes looking for the half chance, for he must be ready to field EVERY ball bowled. Not that he ever has to do this, but he must be ready to take every ball, ready to leap to right or left like a flash of lightning.

Yes, the stumper certainly must be a specialist, a fellow with a great enthusiasm for the game, a real zeal for hard work and a willingness to take knocks.

The keeper must have the eye of a hawk and a brain that acts with instantaneous speed, for standing behind the stumps calls for the expert co-ordination of mind, limb and muscle. Any slacking on the part of the keeper will very quickly show itself in the total of "Mr. Extras."

I think it only right to point out here, however, that the score of "Mr. Extras" does not always accurately reflect the work of the wicket keeper. Even the best stumper has an off day sometimes, so don't worry if there are occasions when your gloves appear to be coated with butter. At the same time, a big total of extras may often be accounted for by erratic bowling or a wearing wicket on which the ball does unaccountable things after pitching, for even in County cricket wickets sometimes cut up badly on the third day of a match.

A first-class stumper can prove an inspiration to the rest of his team, and a deterrent to the batsmen. Knowing that he has a smart keeper behind him curbs a batsman's natural impetuosity and keeps him in his place. I was always somewhat subdued when I had one of cricket's great stumpers behind me, for with such men it is folly for the batsman to attempt to take a risk of any sort.

When I speak of a good wicket keeper I am not referring to the fellow who boasts that he "stands up" to all types of bowlers. When I hear a statement like that I always laugh. Not that I deprecate anyone thinking he's good—if he IS good—but a stumper who stands up to ALL bowlers is not a good stumper.

The best wicket keepers invariably stand well back to the pace men for several reasons; (1) it is best to get as good a sight of a fast ball as possible, especially when it is swinging to any degree; (2) if a ball shoots, the keeper has little chance of stopping it and in these days when the position of "long stop" is considered archaic, four byes will most likely be the result; (3) standing close up to a fast bowler gives a stumper little chance of making a catch off a snick; but standing back gives every chance.

With regard to stumping, how often do you find a batsman stumped off a pace bowler? Hardly ever, so on that score the stumper need not worry about missing anything if he stands back. There is little to gain by

105

crouching right over the stumps when there is a bowler of any pace at the other end.

For all bowlers other than the speedsters by all means stand well up to the stumps and take everything that comes your way.

Now I will repeat to wicket keepers what I have already advised batsmen and bowlers—watch the star men at work and you should pick up innumerable hints that will be of assistance to you when next you don the pads and gloves, for the great stumper has only reached eminence because he has made a concentrated study of his job.

One thing you will notice about all these first-class keepers: there is no unnecessary flourish or showiness about their work. They do their job in a quiet, workman-like manner, but there is something confident and safe about everything they do. Watch a man like Tommy Wade, of Essex, one of the quietest chaps I know, but one of the soundest stumpers in the game. Godfrey Evans, the Kent and England keeper, is another of the same type. He gained his place in the Test team because he proved that he was a worker and not just a showpiece.

By the way, if you feel you would benefit from coaching or advice in your specialist's job, go to a wicket keeper who has gained his knowledge from hard won experience.

To continue, the good stumper is worth his place in the team even although he never scores a run with the bat. The runs he saves, the catches he takes, the confidence he gives to the rest of the side will amply make up for his lack of success with the bat. If, as captain of a side, I had to choose between a player who was a poor stumper but a good bat and one who was a poor bat but a brilliant stumper, I should give the position to the latter. No team can expect success unless the man behind the stumps knows everything there is to know about his job.

It is often said that the looker-on sees most. This is true of the keeper, and if he is a keen student of the game, he can prove his worth by putting his eyes and his brain to good use. He is in a position to weigh up the batsmen in front of him better than any other member of the fielding side. He can also see the full effect of the bowlers' work, which makes it possible for him to advise the captain or the bowlers accordingly.

Many a batsman has been dismissed because the stumper has noticed some weakness in his play and has passed on the tip to the bowler, who has made the most of the advice. That is a very good illustration of the way the keeper can play his full part in dictating the team's attacking strategy.

The stumper should never hesitate to appeal—but only when he is sure that the batsman is out. If you wear the gloves, don't make your voice a nuisance. I have seen fellows who seem to have the idea that they should appeal after nearly every ball. This sort of keeper only jars on everyone's nerves—the umpire's especially. So play fair.

Here is another point to watch. Don't talk to the batsman while he's shaping up for a ball, in an effort to put him off his stroke. That is not cricket.

As a young County player I remember a wicket keeper in one particular match constantly telling me of the wizardry of his bowling team-mate.

"By jove, he can spin that ball," he would say. "He's hot-stuff. He's bowled all the best batsmen in the game."

Every time I shaped for a shot I would hear the stumper muttering to me, knowing that I was young to the game and might be put off. At last, just as the bowler was about

H*

to make his run up, I stepped back from the wicket and turned my head away.

The umpire instantly enquired the reason, and I was not slow to tell him, with the result that the keeper was advised very bluntly to keep his tongue still.

That caution certainly quietened him and I was able to concentrate on my batting. I was a little concerned at the time about my action, but in the pavilion afterwards we were discussing it and I was relieved to hear Johnnie Douglas, our skipper, and some of the older professionals agree that I had done the right thing.

The good wicket keeper does not need to stoop to such tactics in an effort to quicken the batsman's dismissal. If he does his work soundly, the chap with the bat will not be able to take chances.

Play fair, and in this connection, don't encroach by taking the ball in front of the stumps. No matter how slowly it is moving, wait for it until it has passed the bat and the stumps.

Here's another small but important point. Don't fidget about behind the stumps. This can put a batsman off his stroke—it can also spoil the slips' clear sight of the ball which is so necessary.

Remember that you have slips behind you and show them every consideration. For instance, don't dive after a ball that is well out of your reach and moving towards first slip. Allow them to take their full part in the game and don't poach upon their province. That is not good team work.

The value to a side of a capable stumper is immeasurable. Recall all the great teams of past years and you will find that each had a first-class man behind the stumps. I have had the pleasure of batting in front of most of the great stumpers since 1921, but of them all, among County keepers, I should say that the most completely competent was Harry Elliott, of Derbyshire. To my mind he stood out on his own for consistency, for he was sound in everything he did. He was an artist in his own particular sphere of cricket.

Then there was wee George Duckworth, of Lancashire and England, the little man with the loud voice. He was as agile as a cat behind the sticks and some of his acrobatic saves were amazing.

The greatest keeper I ever saw, however, was Bert Oldfield, of Australia. All the best cricket judges agree that Oldfield had everything. There was never anything showy about him, and at times it hardly seemed that there was a man behind the stumps when the Australians were in the field, for he was so unobtrusive. But he was greased lightning when a half chance of a catch or a split second stumping presented itself. In 37 Tests against England, Bert Oldfield dismissed 90 batsmen, a wonderful testimonial to his work.

The agility of some of these human Jacks-in-the-box has always amazed me. I remember an astonishing incident that caused my own dismissal. It was in a match at Southend, against Derbyshire. When my score stood at 99, Tom Mitchell sent down a wide ball on the leg side. I spun round quickly and gave it the stick as hard as I could. But Harry Elliott had anticipated the delivery and leapt across to gather the ball.

Unfortunately, I connected with the ball and slammed it like a bullet straight into his stomach. Poor Harry rolled over, writhing with pain—but he was still gripping the ball. I was out, and so was Harry Elliott. He followed me into the pavilion, only semi-conscious.

The point is this, however, I was caught out through the wonderful anticipation and lightning alertness of the stumper in getting across to take that over-pitched ball on the leg.

If you fancy adopting the position of wicket keeper, you'll need plenty of courage, but it will give you added confidence if you are well protected. Always wear a wicket keeper's body protector, a good pair of pads and the best gloves you can buy. Some of the stumpers I have met have also protected the tips of their fingers with adhesive tape.

Take no chances with your hands and your body, for if you are laid out, your position will not easily be filled by a substitute.

Above all, show patience. The batsman won't always run down the pitch to present you with easy stumpings, and you cannot expect the chance of a catch every over. Good batsmen, too, don't allow much to pass the bat and when this happens the impatient stumper is inclined to get a little ruffled. My advice to you stumpers is, have patience and your chance will come.

Give of your best. Concentrate hard all the time. Take the ball cleanly and smartly, and remember, it is better to be safe than sorry.

X

The Leader of the Team

I FEEL this book would not be complete without a few words about captains and captaincy, for the leadership of a cricket team carries with it a load of responsibility.

First and foremost, the captain must have an unimpeachable character and personality, for he can do a great deal towards promoting the proper team spirit. He must know his men, know their cricket capabilities and their varying temperaments, which play such an important part in cricket, and he must do everything in his power to mould those temperaments into one harmonious whole. For harmony brings success.

The team captain should have a very thorough and comprehensive knowledge of the game and be always ready to set an example to his men, especially in the field. He should never hesitate to make quick and frequent bowling changes in times of emergency. He should allow his bowlers to set their own field and then give them his full support in whatever they think fit to do, for they, like him, will have the team's interest at heart—or they should have. At the same time, the captain must have the last word, and if he feels that a bowler would do well to change his tactics in opposition to any particular batsman, because of something that he has noticed, then he should take the step.

One thing I do not like to see, however. Some teams have an abundance of bowlers and I have known captains who have given every one of those trundlers a chance to bowl an over or two, not because they were worthy of the chance, but just for the sake of keeping their interest keyed-up. That is definitely wrong. The good captain sticks to his regular bowlers and only calls on the others when the stock men have failed. Remember, the skipper should show neither fear nor favour.

Another important duty of a skipper, of course, is to decide whether to bat if he wins the toss. Some captains think this is the be-all and the end-all of their position, but that is far from being true. However, the winning of the toss throws a big responsibility upon the skipper, for it is so easy to make a mistake in his choice, a mistake which will not make itself apparent until it is too late. Many matches have been won and lost upon the captain's decision after winning the toss of the coin.

Should he be in any doubt about the wisdom of batting on a wicket that may play tricks, the skipper should not be afraid to ask the advice of his senior player, or a team member with more experience than his own. That happens often in the County game, and even in Test cricket, too. I do not suggest that the captain should throw the onus of such a decision upon other shoulders, but two heads are usually better than one in such instances.

On the field the good captain is watching his men all the time, and his opponents, too, of course, and is constantly thinking and scheming. He must never relax his concentration. He must be the team's leader not only in name.

For instance, fielders often wander out of position— some even doze off during an innings! It is up to the skipper to call them to order.

Johnnie Douglas, the Essex skipper during my early years with the County, was a great captain, a hard task-master maybe, but he was such a keen cricketer himself that he would not countenance the slightest slacking by any of his men. He was ready and willing to put everything he had into the game, and he expected every one of us to do the same. No one could blame him for that, for like all really great captains, he never shirked the responsibility for anything that happened on the field.

Off the field he was just the same, for he was jealous for the reputation of cricket, and especially that of the County.

Percy Fender, of Surrey, was another of the great leaders of cricket under whom I had the pleasure of playing. P. G. H. was such a capable leader that I always considered him unfortunate in not being chosen to lead an England side. He knew how to get the best out of his men and the harmonious family spirit was always in evidence whenever he was skippering a side.

Arthur Gilligan, of Sussex and England; R. K. Nunes (West Indies); "Nummy" Deane and Alan Melville, both of South Africa, and not forgetting Don Bradman, of Australia; these were other ideal skippers, men who were natural leaders.

Some teams, of course, have the right team spirit so well developed that they hardly need a captain, except to carry out the elementary duties of the skipper, but whenever you find a good sound team who reveal all the best aspects of cricket in its widest form, you will find them led by a man who knows the value of harmony and does everything to foster it.

Give your skipper your interest and support both on and off the field, and you will find, as I always found, that your cricket will be far more enjoyable.

XI

Cricket the Greatest Game of all

WE ARE fast approaching the end of our chat on cricket, but after delving into my store of memories and endeavouring to pass on advice and opinions formed during many years in the game, I am still convinced that I shall never know all there is to know about cricket.

Just as I told you earlier in this book that no cricketer can ever attain perfection, I am quite certain that no player will ever possess a complete practical knowledge of cricket in all its many phases. That does not mean to say, however, that young players cannot try to achieve that end. The cricketer who endeavours to reach perfection, both actively and mentally, is more likely to climb to the heights than the fellow who is content to remain just an ordinary player with little ambition.

Throughout our chat I have tried to tell you how I think the game should be played and the spirit that should be developed if you are to derive full satisfaction from your achievements on the cricket field. Yet there is one aspect of the game which we have not yet discussed, and that is a knowledge of the laws of cricket.

"Oh, the laws of cricket," you may say, "but surely there are too many of them for anyone to learn and digest them all thoroughly?"

Perhaps you are right, although I am not saying that I fully agree with you, but that does not excuse any cricketer for not having a sound knowledge of the main laws, that is to say, the general laws that apply in almost

114

every match that is played. To be a good sound cricketer you MUST know the laws.

I do not intend to discuss those laws here, for most of them are self-explanatory, but every player should know enough about them to be able to "stand" as umpire. In junior club cricket it is often necessary for the players to take it in turns to don the white coat, and there is nothing more likely to spoil the harmonious spirit of a game than to have umpires who do not know enough about the game to give sound decisions. Don't you agree?

Just a few words then about umpires and umpiring.

The laws of cricket state that there shall be an umpire for each end—for each end and not for each side. In other words, the umpire should be strictly fair in everything he does, showing no favour to either side. It may be a great temptation for a player-umpire to refuse the appeal of the bowler who has legitimately beaten his pal, maybe the team's best batsman, but cricket's popularity has been founded upon an unimpeachable sporting spirit.

If you are asked to "stand," remember that the two umpires are in charge of the game. Show confidence in everything you do; make your decisions quickly, confidently and firmly, but not in any dictatorial manner. Having given a decision, then stick to it and do not argue with the players on any pretext. If a player asks you a question, by all means give him a straight answer, but do not hold any discussion upon your decisions. Actually, of course, if the players have the right spirit they will not question a decision, whatever they think about its validity.

Learn the correct signals and make them clearly and firmly to the scorers. If you are called upon to "no-ball" a bowler, shout "No ball!" the moment the delivery is made to give the batsman a chance to deal with the ball as it should be dealt with.

Watch every ball and every stroke, whether it is at your end or not, for the two umpires should work in co-operation, always ready to give a decision when there is any doubt in the mind of the fellow at the other end. This is sometimes necessary when a catch is made on the "blind side" of an umpire. But never interfere with your opposite number unless he asks for your co-operation in making a decision.

You may be criticised for some of your decisions, but if you feel you are right, then stand on your own legs, for you are in charge. For that reason do not hesitate to challenge any player who, in your opinion is guilty of committing an unsporting action.

An incident of that nature happened in a County game. A well-known batsman deliberately kicked away a ball that pitched well outside his off stump. It rolled away towards third man and the batsman called to his partner and started to run.

But that run was not completed. The umpire instantly called back the man who had kicked the ball.

"Back you go," he said. "You can't score runs that way. Play fair."

Some of the players and many of the spectators thought the umpire was overstepping his authority, but after all, if the umpire thought that the batsman's action was unsporting—and it was—he was in duty bound to assert his legitimate authority.

Another umpire incident comes to mind. It was in a match between Essex and Lancashire. I was batting at one end and my skipper, J. W. H. T. Douglas, was at the other. Ted MacDonald, the former Australian Test star, was the bowler and on a hard wicket his express deliveries were getting up about our ears. One ball shot up like a rocket, cracked Johnnie Douglas on the head and ricochetted to cover point, where Harry Makepeace brought off a smart catch.

Meanwhile the Essex skipper had fallen to the turf, knocked out by that fierce delivery. Some minutes later he recovered sufficiently to take up his bat and, with that dogged Douglas look on his bronzed features, he prepared to resume his innings, although there was an ugly swelling on the side of his head. But I shall never forget the look on his face when he heard the umpire say:

"Sorry, Mr. Douglas, you were out—caught."

Poor Johnnie was dumbstruck. He could not believe it, for he was under the impression that he had been given out caught off his head. But the umpire adhered to his decision and Essex had lost another wicket.

Now the umpire was quite right in his decision. You see, when the ball rose head high, Johnnie Douglas threw up his hand to protect his face. The ball struck his glove, bounced on to his head and then into the hands of cover point. It needed courage to give such a decision, for our skipper was one of the greatest personalities in cricket, but it was perfectly fair and correct. It would have been unfair to our opponents from Lancashire if any other decision had been given.

I have met young players who have not relished a spell of umpiring, but if you are offered the chance to "stand," take it. It will be an experience that will help to increase your knowledge of the game and to develop your confidence and your sense of responsibility.

I want now to pass quickly to the training necessary for cricket. As a matter of fact, cricket is not like some other games, football for instance, so far as physical training is concerned; nevertheless, the young player with ambition should not neglect to give thought to his own personal fitness.

During the cricket season he should lead a steady life and do nothing that would impair his wind or his eye. No late nights just prior to an important match, for instance. But what about the winter months, you may ask?

It is quite common for young cricketers to put their cricket gear away after their last match and think no more about the game until the spring approaches. That is quite all right, providing those fellows indulge in some other fairly strenuous sport during the winter

It was always impressed upon me as a lad that I should never spend an idle winter if I wanted to maintain my form, and throughout my cricket career I was always active during the close season, playing squash and badminton and taking long walks whenever possible. Thus I kept my muscles and my eyes tuned up all the time. Had I spent my winters in idleness, I doubt whether I should have retained my fitness for so many years.

If you are inactive for any length of time, your muscles stiffen and when the cricket season recommences it takes you longer to get back into the swing of things. When that happens you may lose your place to a fitter player and be unable to regain it.

Many young players hamper their progress through idle winters, so don't let this happen to you. Keep on the go all the time. Prepare for your summer's cricket during the winter months and you will take an active part in cricket for many years to come.

Cricket is such a grand game—to my mind the greatest

of all—that it deserves all that you can put into it. I have never regretted adopting it as my career and for that reason I should like to offer a short word of advice to any of you who have such a profound interest in the game that you feel you would give a great deal to play cricket professionally.

If you cherish such an ambition and have the necessary capabilities and mental outlook, then by all means go all out to achieve your ambition. But cricket must be more than just a pleasant recreation to you, for you must be prepared to work really hard and to take all the many ups and downs that will be your lot as a County cricketer.

The chance to make cricket your profession is not likely to come to you, however, unless you reveal the right degree of determination. No lad with an inferiority complex will make a first-class cricketer, but there is an old adage which says that "a man can do what he thinks he can do." So if you feel that you could make a success of a cricket career, then by all means fight for your chance.

The Counties are always on the look out for promising lads and never hesitate to offer trials to earnest applicants. Your application for such a trial will be fairly considered. I have seen hundreds of young players given a trial with one or another of the County clubs; not all have blossomed into first-class cricketers, of course, but many have. So if you are seriously considering cricket as a career, then don't hesitate to apply to your own County for a chance to prove your merits.

The adoption of any career is a gamble, and cricket, like so many sports, is more precarious, perhaps, than life on an office stool or in a workshop, but the lad who has not the self-confidence and the determination to take a chance is never likely to make much of his life in any sphere.

Don't think of a cricket career, however, if you are looking for an easy life, for you will not achieve your desire. But with hard work, confidence and the right outlook that will allow you to take the rough with the smooth, plus your fair share of luck, of course, you should make good. Once you are established, then I know you will be able to say with me that there is no better life.

Cricket has been my whole life and I have no regrets. I only wish I could live it all again. It hasn't always been easy, but I have enjoyed every moment of my years in first-class cricket, for the life has enabled me to see far more of the world and to make many more very good friends than I should have done had I chosen a business or industrial career.

There are no fortunes to be made in cricket, I can assure you of that, but to my mind the personal satisfaction and the enjoyment I have derived from the game more than outweigh the financial aspect.

It was cricket that gave me one of the greatest thrills that any man could experience. It happened in 1929 at Weston-super-Mare, where I was playing for Essex against Somerset. It was just an ordinary County Championship match, but it provided a real story book finish.

On the third day Somerset had a good chance of overhauling our score and winning the points, but against some determined bowling and excellent fielding, their wickets fell fast. However, when Bert Luckes, the last man in, walked to the wicket, they needed only two runs to win—and I was the bowler.

My legs were not quite as steady as they should have been as I trotted up to the crease, for I knew that the result of the match depended upon me. One slightly loose ball, one good hit by the batsman and it would all be over.

Down went that ball. It pitched well up, broke viciously and Luckes made a swipe at it. Next moment I leapt into the air in my joy, for the leg peg was lolling over and the bails were on the turf. Luckes was out!

Essex had snatched victory by a mere two runs and I had dismissed five Somerset batsmen for 25 runs. That was the biggest thrill of my whole cricket life and certainly one of my brightest memories.

But the finish of all matches were not quite so serious as that one.

Some years ago, for instance, we were playing Lancashire at Leyton, and when stumps were drawn at the end of the second day's play, the Northerners needed just TWO runs for victory. No extra time was permissible on the second day, so in consequence we had to turn out again on the following morning in order that the men from Lancashire could score the necessary runs.

That day's play consisted of exactly two balls, off the second of which four runs were scored, giving Lancashire victory. But I shall never forget walking out on to the Leyton pitch that morning, watched by not more than four spectators—and they were the groundsmen. What a laugh they must have got, for we Essex players were wearing our civvy togs. Some of the players wore bowler hats, while Nichols was clad in plus fours. The umpires were decked out in their white coats and the two Lancashire batsmen were wearing their flannels and looked as though they were prepared to bat all day if need be. Two balls were enough and the match was all over.

More and more memories flood upon me, but I cannot dwell upon them any longer, except to recall some of the greatest contemporary players of my time. From among them I have tried to select my ideal team. This was far from simple, for there were so many outstanding cricket personalities during the years between the two wars, and the choice of only eleven men to form a complete team, taking into account all that is necessary in the building of a team, meant leaving out many of the stars. However, here are the men I have selected for my ideal team.

For the opening pair, Hobbs and Sutcliffe choose themselves. It would be impossible to leave them out of any side. For No. 3 I was torn between Frank Woolley, the masterly Kent left-hander, and Wally Hammond, but I have chosen Hammond, on his day England's most complete run-getter and the world's greatest slip fielder and also a class bowler. For No. 4—Patsy Hendren, wonderful hitter of hundreds, grand deep fielder and the most meteoric personality I ever met on the cricket field. Next comes Maurice Leyland, the little Yorkshireman, an all-rounder without an equal; followed by P. G. H. Fender, dashing batsman, bowler and fielder, but worthy of his place in any side for his brilliant captaincy.

Another all-rounder comes next—my old Essex comrade Morris Nichols, chosen by me not out of any sentiment but because of his capacity for bowling all day in emergency. He would be my stock bowler. For wicket keeper I choose Harry Elliott, of Derbyshire, and then come the three greatest bowlers of my time, Maurice Tate, Harold Larwood, and "Tich" Freeman.

Well, then, there is my ideal team of a past era—Hobbs, Sutcliffe, Hammond, Hendren, Leyland, Fender, Nichols, Elliott, Larwood, Tate and Freeman—personality skipper, five magnificent batsmen, three all-rounders, an attack comprising seven bowlers, a wonderful stumper, and the whole eleven sound and safe in the field, for never forget that the work of good batsmen and bowlers would be wasted if the fielding was not up to the same high standard.

Now some of you will be saying: "But what about the stars of to-day?" so I will satisfy you by suggesting that the best side that could be selected from players of this era would be: Hutton, Washbrook, Edrich, Compton, Hardstaff, Norman Yardley (captain), Ikin, Cranston, Evans, Wright and Copson.

As with the team of "old 'uns," if I may be permitted to term them such, here you have another side of grand batsmen, brilliant bowlers and alert fielders. Compare the two sides if you like, but I refrain from doing so. Too many old players contend that the cricketers of their day were better than their modern counterparts. I am not here to argue the point, and the only way to prove the contention would be to place the two teams I have chosen in direct opposition on the cricket field—which is impossible.

There is nothing wrong with modern cricket, and the future, to my mind, is bright. The players are there in as great array as ever and many more—yes, more than ever before—are on the threshold of fame, waiting for their big chance.

My own playing days are rapidly drawing to a close and I am now mainly concerned with trying to "produce" well-coached youth to follow in the footsteps of that galaxy of great men who have passed across the cricket stage. I take justifiable pride in the deeds of some of the players I have helped up the first rungs of the ladder.

I have seen many of the present Essex team step into prominence—Peter Smith, Tommy Wade, Alf Avery and

Stan Cray in particular. At Eton, I have been privileged to assist in the cricket education of many fine young players, including the Hon. L. R. White, who played for England against Australia in a war-time Test; Keighley, now with Yorkshire; Blake, a grand bat who should make a name with Sussex; and last year's captain, Rudd, son of the famous runner. This capable young batsman's departure for South Africa may mean that we shall not see much of him in English cricket; more's the pity.

These then are young players who are on the road to stardom, and many others are preparing to follow them.

There is a great pride of achievement in playing first-class cricket, but although it is only natural for a man to regret the passing of the most active years of his life, I shall always be happy if I can continue to try to impart my own knowledge, gained from long experience in the game, to the young men who will uphold cricket's great traditions in the future. No man could ask for more from life, and if I have been able to help YOU to a deeper interest in the game and to a clearer conception of some of its finer points, I am content.

Good luck to you all, and good cricket.